The Paradise of All These Parts

ALSO BY JOHN HANSON MITCHELL

The Rose Café: Love and War in Corsica

Looking for Mr. Gilbert: The Reimagined Life of an African American

Following the Sun: A Bicycle Pilgrimage from Andalusia to the Hebrides

The Wildest Place on Earth: Italian Gardens and the Invention of Wilderness

Trespassing: An Inquiry into the Private Ownership of Land

Walking Towards Walden: A Pilgrimage in Search of Place

A Field Guide to Your Own Back Yard

Ceremonial Time: Fifteen Thousand Years on One Square Mile

The Paradise of All These Parts

A Natural History of Boston

John Hanson Mitchell

BEACON PRESS, BOSTON

Beacon Press
Boston, Massachusetts
www.beacon.org

Beacon Press books
are published under the auspices of
the Unitarian Universalist Association of Congregations.

20 19 18 17   8 7 6 5 4 3 2

This book is printed on acid-free paper that meets the uncoated paper ANSI/NISO specifications for permanence as revised in 1992.

Text design by Susan E. Kelly
of Wilsted & Taylor Publishing Services

Library of Congress Cataloging-in-Publication Data

Mitchell, John Hanson.
The paradise of all these parts : a natural history of Boston / John Hanson Mitchell.
p. cm.
ISBN 978-0-8070-7149-6 (pbk.)
1. Natural history—Massachusetts—Boston. 2. Boston (Mass.)—History.
3. Urban ecology—Massachusetts—Boston. I. Title.

QH105.M4M58 2008
508.744'61—dc22   2007045467

For Kai

"Success to the crooked but interesting town of Boston"
—Inscription on an eighteenth-century English pitcher

Contents

Preface

For years now I have been interested in the question of what the Spanish call *querencia,* which, loosely translated, means something like sense of place, or a personal intimacy with a singular region. Those with a strong feeling of querencia will know the weather of their country, will know the dates of the arrivals and departures of local migratory birds, and the flowerings of trees and shrubs. They will be familiar with the courses and names of local rivers and streams, the dates of the seasonal passages of fish, and the location of hidden animal trails, of dens, swamps, hollows, cliffs, and odd boulders or outcroppings. Furthermore, they will know that certain sites within their terrain exhibit almost mystical emanations. Things seem to happen unexpectedly in these particular places. Over the years the sites assume an identity of their own and become part of the continuing narrative of the region. Sometimes such areas may even enter into national or world history.

One has to wonder, however, why it is that certain human communities on earth breed a strong sense of querencia, whereas other spots engender little more than a bored indifference. Why do certain places emerge from inhuman wilderness tracts and become powerful cities or historic towns? Why should an obscure bend on the Thames River become London, for example, or a small island on the river Seine become the heart of the city of Paris? Why Athens? Why Rome? Why, for that matter, Boston?

Having knocked about a bit in various port cities of the world, and having happened upon Boston, it seemed to me that the city had a definitive sense of itself, a certain pride of place. I learned later that from its very beginnings this characteristic was evident, even predicted. The explorer John Smith called the place "the Paradise of all these parts" when he first sailed into the harbor in 1614, and Boston's first governor, John Winthrop, in the famous sermon delivered to his Puritan flock on board the *Arbella,* proclaimed that their new settlement would be as a city on a hill: the eyes of all the world would be watching. And as it turned out, in time the little peninsula upon which the town was built became, at least in the eyes of its citizens, the veritable Hub of the known world, the Athens of America. Boston evolved into the quintessential American place, exhibiting, as we are taught in school (or were once, anyway), the best of the American vision. As any passerby along Tremont Street on the east side of the Common will be told, this is the spot where the American story begins.

Much of this pride of place over the three and half centuries of English and American occupancy has been expressed in literature and art. Boston was settled by a highly literate people and for this reason happens to be one of the best-documented places in the United States as far as politics, religion, war, philosophy, literature, art, music, and architecture are concerned. Curiously, however, one of the least-documented aspects of the city's history is the actual nature of the place. This is an odd omission. The city would not exist were it not for its deep-water harbor and navigable rivers, its sharp hills underlain by water-bearing gravel beds, its abundance of fish and waterfowl and its nearby wooded hills. Furthermore, thanks partly to its libraries and universities, Boston developed into an important center for the study of the natural sciences, and later, starting around 1850, became the epicenter of the nascent American environmental movement.

There are many published works on the human history of the city, as well any number of guidebooks to its architecture, streets, and parks, but in spite of Boston's inherent connection to the natural world, there has yet to be a book that deals with the deeper story—a history of its rocks and rivers, its hills and hollows, trees and shrubs, and the wild animals that once inhabited these shores.

With this in mind, having learned a little bit about the local environment over the thirty-five years that I have lived in the area, I set out to fill the gap.

The Paradise of All These Parts

CHAPTER ONE

A Short Walk on the Shawmut

The Place That Was Boston

ON A BRIGHT DAY in early September, when the morning was fresh and sweet, and the goldenrods and asters were all abloom, and everywhere in thickets and field edges and woodlots the little white-throated sparrows were whistling, I set out on a short walk around the old Shawmut Peninsula. My intention that day was to see if I could circumambulate the boundaries of the original town of Boston by following the primordial shoreline of the little spit of upland upon which the city was built. But suffice it to say that the venture was doomed from the start. There have been any number of changes in the topography of the peninsula since those unrecorded days in the sixteenth century when the first European voyagers discovered the harbor, and in the end I was forced onto city streets, exposed to dangerous traffic, swept up by rushing herds of commuters, and assailed by noise and noxious fumes. But never mind, armed solely with naive ambition, I set out.

Boston in our time is a great, sprawling port city, stacked with the towering monuments of commercial accomplishment and set on the northwestern edge of a large bay dotted with many green islands. Seen from the height of one of these towers or from the window of a descending airliner, the town appears to roll out west, north, and south in a gray-green landscape of developed land that feathers gently into a vast leafy forest stretching south to the slopes of the Great Blue Hill and west to two eminences, Mount Wachusett and, farther off and standing alone, Mount Monadnock, in New Hampshire. But the built city is an illusion, a later addition to the real bedrock landform that for 14,000 years lay silently on the right bank of a wide tidal river known since colonial times as the Charles. The original Shawmut Peninsula was a tight little island attached to the mainland by a narrow neck and remarkable primarily for a series of sharp hills that were visible to mariners from far out at sea.

My walkabout over this aboriginal landscape that day had a significant beginning on several levels. In a reversal of the epic journeys of classical literature, in which, after many adventures, the hero descends into the Underworld, on that fateful morning I had struggled upward through a labyrinth of dark tunnels, emerged from the Underworld at the Park Street T station, and burst into the upper airs of John Winthrop's celestial city on a hill. Here, under the translucent morning sky, I began my walk in the very place where, in a sense, the recorded story of Boston began—on the original cow common. It was on Beacon Hill that the misanthropic Anglican clergyman William Blackstone, the first permanent European resident of the Shawmut Peninsula, settled in 1625.

Blackstone was a slightly eccentric character, the first of many who would later inhabit this place. He rode around the countryside on the back of a brindle bull, lived alone in his English thatched cottage, and kept a few cows, a herd of pigs, and a vegetable garden, and, in another enduring characteristic of the site, he maintained a library of more than 180 books. He had come over with a company of Anglican adventurers headed by Robert Gorges in 1623 that settled temporarily south of the Shawmut, near Quincy. In less than two years, having had a taste of two New England winters, Gorges gave up and returned to England, but for reasons known only to himself, Blackstone chose to remain. He moved up to the peninsula and eventually established himself on its western slope, just above the mouth of the Charles River. Five years later the *Arbella* landed with a company of Puritan settlers under the leadership of the colony's first governor, John Winthrop, and at Blackstone's invitation, settled on the peninsula and renamed the place Boston.

All that came very late in the geographic history of this little patch of the North American coast, however. The real story begins with the land. In fact the real story begins in the Underworld, wherein lies the evidence of the elemental forces that formed this particular place. Just beyond the tiled walls of the Boston subway system lies the dark matter that makes up the real foundation upon which the celestial city was built. Geologist friends of mine, whose time lines tend to run in millions of years, explain that construction of the subway system, later excavations for the Boston Common Parking Garage and Center Plaza, and, most especially, work on the aptly named Big Dig and its harbor tunnels, encountered a deep bed of shale, forged more than 600 million years ago, when the general landscape around Boston was characterized by a massive chain of volcanoes and associated earthquakes and mudslides. The ever-changing patterns of the earth's crust and the upheavals of vast, eruptive volcanoes and sinking terranes created, among other landforms, an immense depression in this region known as the Boston Basin. Over the eons, rains fell; rivers streamed down from the rising continent; the very earth shifted in its orbit around the sun; the climate cooled; and immense plates of ice came scraping down out of the north and then retreated. Seas fell away and rose again, and then, in the final act of stage setting, a tiny band of people from Siberia followed the walls of receding glacial ice northward and began settling in temporary hunting camps on top of the hills that the glacier left behind.

For the first 15,000 years of its dry-land existence, the tadpole-shaped strip of land that became Boston was characterized by these sharp little glacial hills—Copp's Hill, Fort Hill, Pemberton, Mount Vernon, and, of course, Beacon Hill, the highest of them all. Then, in the autumn of 1630, John Winthrop and his company of Puritans moved across the Charles River to the Shawmut Peninsula. Unlike Blackstone, who chose to live with nature rather than contrary to it, the Puritans began to remake the place shortly after they landed. They cleared the native forest that had supported Blackstone's herd of swine. They constructed lanes, then streets, then a "Great Highwaye to Roxberre." They built docks and tide mills, ferry landings, windmills, and meetinghouses, and when they were done with that, in order to create more dry land they leveled the hills and used the fill to widen the tadpole tail that once connected the peninsula to the mainland. In effect, the Puritans began a process of leveling and filling and digging and delving that is still going on in our time.

Not surprisingly, given his character, Blackstone decamped for the wilds of Rhode Island shortly after the work began.

These distant events, which seem far removed from the traffic and the politics and the hot pulse of contemporary Boston, are not so far removed nor as insignificant as one would think. The native people of this place, the linguistically associated group that came to be known as the Massachusett Indians, chipped their spear points and arrowheads from the volcanic rocks of the nearby Blue Hills. The freshwater spring that bubbled up from ancient gravel beds on Beacon Hill is one of the resources that encouraged the Puritans to settle on the peninsula. And many of the modern buildings that rose up in subsequent centuries were constructed of local granites laid down in a time when all the earth was young and life was just struggling upward out of primordial seas.

September is a fine month for a walk in Boston. From the summit of Beacon Hill above the Common on that bright morning, I could see below me an anomalous wooded landscape, its scrim of lacy branches and leaves nearly obscuring the wall of city buildings rising beyond. In the upper canopy of the city trees, I could see the little darting forms of migrating wood warblers, which had spent the summer in the vast spruce and fir forest of the Laurentian Shield in Canada and now, in late summer, were headed southward for Central America. Lower down, in remnant patches of shrubbery and the flower beds of the Public Garden, the ubiquitous white-throated sparrows were still moving through. I could hear their plaintive little whistles as I made my way along and also hear the rhythmic, bouncing song of goldfinches, the *chuck* of robins, the clucking of flocks of blackbirds, and even the periodic cry of a creamy white-winged gull slipping over the gold dome of the State House.

The leaves of the oaks and maples were just beginning to show the first tinges of autumn, and in spite of the surround of traffic, the air carried a fresh smell of vegetation and old moist earth. Elsewhere in this greening city, honey mushrooms and boletes and meadow mushrooms were forcing their way up out of the soils and logs in those little shrubby patches as yet untended by the vigilant city landscaping crews. Young spiderlings had climbed out onto the edges of leaves, high in the trees, and were paying out strands of gossamer in order to catch the breezes and parachute off to new territories. And even here, in the heart of the city, you might hear the scream of a red-tailed hawk, a species that has returned to the city in recent decades, along with peregrine falcons, owls, and other formerly banished predatory species.

A few late-arriving commuters were hurrying along below me on the paths of the Common. I could see nannies and mothers and au pairs out with their charges, some of whom, I noticed, were proudly pushing their own baby carriages. Tourists were headed south toward the Frog Pond and the Public Garden, and also in evidence that morning, on one of the lawns below the State House, was a group of five or six men and women with bedrolls and backpacks who, for one reason or another, having found themselves without shelter, had spent the night under the stars. These people, I had learned from previous encounters, have an understanding—if not an appreciation—of certain aspects of the natural night life of this city, the rats, bats, owls, raccoons, possums, and other dark creatures that emerge with dusk.

Over the years, the former cow common became the defining characteristic of the Boston mind. It used to be said that a Bostonian's world view was limited to fifty acres—the size of the original Common. And while it is true that the stage sets have changed over the past four hundred or so years, and the cast of characters has shifted decidedly, here under the sheltering trees is a remnant, or at least a hint, of the last of the unmade landscape that was the place the Massachusett Indians called Shawmut.

The Common has been much improved since the 1640s. Under the management of the Puritans, this area became a treeless, barren plot, overgrazed by cows and used for military training and, by way of entertainment, the exhibition of malingerers in stocks and pillories, not to mention the periodic hangings of criminals and witches, as well as those unfortunates who did not happen to agree with the strictures of Puritan doctrine. But the Puritans' descendants, having established themselves comfortably in the place, banished the cows in 1830, ceased the hangings of dissenters and witches, and replanted the parade grounds with elms, oaks, maples, hickories, and other native trees—some of which still survive. On this clear morning, the basketwork of their branches provided a pleasing contrast to the walls of glass and steel beyond.

My plan that day was to make my way across the Common toward the Charles River, cut through the area where Mount Vernon once stood, then turn and head south back through the Public Garden to Park Plaza and the theater district and thence northward through the financial district to the North End. From here my intention was to skirt the harbor and come back to the Common by way of Salem Street.

Roughly speaking, this route would follow the original shoreline of the peninsula, although with all the wharf building and tearing down of hills and filling up of wetlands it would be hard to know exactly where I was. For all I know, had I undertaken this walk in 1630, I would have been forced to walk on water at some points.

The name Shawmut is variously translated from the Algonquian as "land of living fountains," because of the many freshwater springs, or as "land accessible by water" or "place where we land our canoes." This last seems unlikely, since the whole Boston Basin, with its three rivers, must have been accessible by water from many points. For a while the Puritans also used the name Shawmut for their settlement, as Blackstone had. But early on they changed the name to Trimount, or Tremount, for the three sharp hills on the northwestern side of the peninsula. It was only later that they called the place Boston, an appellation borrowed from a town in Lincolnshire, England, whence some of the Puritans had come. Interestingly enough, the British Boston had a reputation for liberality, and in the early part of the seventeenth century it sheltered, albeit briefly, the company of extreme separatists who became known as Pilgrims and in 1620 made their way to Plymouth.

"Tadpole" is perhaps not the best description of the Shawmut Peninsula, in spite the wide seaward-facing head and the narrow tail connecting the land to the continent. Some land-use historians have seen a salamander in the landform, some refer to it as a pear, and along the way, some English settler must have seen a head, since for decades—until it was obliterated by filling—the tail was referred to as the Neck. Others have seen a closed fist, with knuckle-like hills. But perhaps the blobby, rounded shapes of Joan Miró's paintings best describe it. In fact, even "peninsula" is not an apt description, since the neck or tail commonly flooded at high tides and was swept by storm surges, creating a temporary island.

The hills were the most impressive characteristic of the place. One of these, Beacon Hill, was high enough to be seen from miles out at sea, and early in its English phase, it was the site of a literal beacon that helped guide ships. Beacon Hill was flanked on the west and east by Mount Vernon and Pemberton Hill. The three hills were steep, and as early as 1633 they were described as grass-covered, the trees having been stripped for fuel and house construction. The nearby islands in the harbor were thickly wooded, although some had been cleared by the Indians. When John Smith arrived, many of them were laid out with gardens of native corn, beans, and squash.

It is likely that earlier the whole Shawmut Peninsula was forested and interspersed with sinks and wet hollows where frogs and salamanders lurked. These murky freshwater wetlands must have resounded with music in early spring when the ice melted back and the wood frogs and spring peepers and toads began to sing. Their songs, which were among the earliest voices of the primordial peninsula, can be heard even today, according to one of my sources, a man named Earl, who sometimes sleeps on the Common. He described to me a sound like sleigh bells ringing from the empty sky that he had heard one night in spring: "I'm thinking Santa Claus is coming," he told me. "Then I remember it's spring and I don't know what the hell's going on."

The bells, I determined after some questioning, were the collective calls of spring peepers, tiny, two-inch-long tree frogs, which elsewhere in Boston have been recorded calling every month of the year, including January.

In the seventeenth century, the hilly northern slopes of the landform were covered with native wildflowers, as well as blueberries and what the English called whortleberries, a European species closely related to huckleberries. One early record, written by Susan Pollard, the first white woman to set foot on the peninsula, described brushy hillsides, swamps, rough terrain, and vegetated hollows. Better records of the plants of the period come later, from an odd source—namely the privy of one Katherine Nanny Naylor, an upright citizen of the early settlement who lived on Cross Street in the North End in the late 1600s.

During an archeological survey for the Central Artery Project, researchers uncovered the privy of the household of Mistress Nanny Naylor and from their findings were able to piece together a sense of what life was like for those who had settled here.

Katherine Nanny Naylor was born in England in 1630 and died in Boston in 1715. Around 1650 she married a rich merchant named Robert Nanny, and when he died after a few years of marriage, she married Edward Naylor. Brother Naylor, although rich from trade in the West Indies, was what we might term today an abusive husband—an admittedly relative term for a man who lived in an era when women were viewed as chattel and there was a strong movement among Boston Puritans for women to be veiled in public. But old man Naylor was violent enough to have brought down the heavy weapons of Puritan law upon his property. We know all this, not from the archeological dig but from court records. Katherine Nanny

Naylor petitioned the General Court for a divorce from Edward. The documents outline the abuses she and her children endured. Among other things, he kicked one child down a set of stairs. He also engaged in dalliances with his female servants. The court sided with Katherine, and she lived for the next thirty years on Cross Street, where the privy was uncovered.

Artifacts found in the privy suggest that she had a good life, her aggressive husband notwithstanding. Archeologists turned up silk and lace, as well as ceramics and glass from Italy and Spain. Also spices from the East Indies and olive pits, and even an old bowling ball. But more to the point for this little history, along with the seeds of cherries and the remains of insects, the archeologists discovered pollen grains, and from these, a specialized group of botanists known as palynologists—who are able to identify plants from their pollen alone—were able to ascertain that between 1650 and 1700, at least, aspen, birch, oak, and maple, as well as hickory and elm, were growing in the vicinity of the early city. All of these plants can still be found on the peninsula, although no doubt not in the abundance in which they were found in 1650.

All in all, before 1630 Boston must have offered an idyllic landscape as seen from the islanded harbor, with blue waters in the foreground, the green eminences of the Shawmut hills beyond, perhaps the smokes of a few Indian cooking fires rising into the sky, open marshes and a hilly mainland clothed with scented forests, and in some sections fields of corn and squashes of the native people who every summer came to this coast to fish and farm.

However, official written descriptions of precolonial Shawmut, mainly the record of John Smith, come very late in the ages of European discovery. The earliest records are conjectural. In the winter of 1003, the Viking ship of Thorfinn Thordarson, in company with two other ships, wintered south of Greenland, somewhere around the Gulf of Saint Lawrence and Chaleur Bay. In the spring the little fleet pushed southward and came to a section of the coast they called "the land of Hop." The term translates to something like "land-locked bay" or "sheltered harbor" and may well have referred to Massachusetts Bay and Boston Harbor.

There is no verifiable evidence of Viking settlements around Boston, although a popular legend in the 1920s held that there had been a Norse town on the Charles River named Norumbega. Nor is there any record of the peninsula's discovery by John Cabot, who explored the northeastern American coast in 1497 and may or may not have taken shelter in the many-islanded harbor, either on his first voyage or, more likely, on his second, in 1498, a voyage from which he never returned.

On a subsequent crossing, Cabot's son, Sebastian, landed somewhere along these shores and described a rich land of fruiting trees and berry bushes, an account filled out in later years by imaginative chroniclers who also put in here. According to these late seventeenth-century descriptions (not always among the most trustworthy records), the tight little island that would become Boston was thriving with strawberries, larch, birch, and hazel, as well as pine, spruce, beech, oaks, and elms. There were wild turkeys and martens, strange animals with flattened tails called beavers, and other marvelous creatures, including the "strong-armed beare, large-limmed Molkes [moose], and the tripping Deere," to quote one source. (Never mind that these early explorers also encountered here "the Kingly Lyon" and the fish-tailed sea gods known as Tritons and peppered their maps with images of sea serpents and mermaids.)

Captain John Smith, who anchored in the harbor in 1614, looked over the green shelter of the islands, the hills of Boston, with the mainland ridges of the Boston Basin in the distance, the rich coastal meadows and the rising continent beyond, and thought the place was an Eden of sorts, an earthly version of paradise.

Paradise lost would perhaps be a better description of the place now. Even before I began my circuit, my plan went awry. Traffic, a lack of green parks beyond the Common, construction barriers, a rushing morning populace intent on work, noise, exhaust, the battering-ram, clank and crack of unseen machines created a sharp contrast to the fresh earth I had so recently passed through on the Common.

Just at the corner of Mount Vernon and Charles streets, a man in a Burberry coat rudely brushed my right shoulder and raced on without so much as a fare-thee-well, let alone an apology. A few minutes later, a shirtless running man dashed by, a cell phone clapped to his ear. People concerned with matters other than the enjoyment of nature and the glorious September morning swept past or crossed in front of me or breathed down my neck in pursuit of their intended missions—whatever they may have been. Not two blocks farther along, a crazy man with a plastic garbage bag for a hat stood in the middle of the street cursing at passing cars for no apparent reason, and at one point my course was blocked outright as a white delivery truck, its annoying warning bell clanging, backed across the sidewalk and stopped, forcing pedestrians to take their lives in their hands on the streets in order to get around.

All this commotion so broke my reverie that I temporarily deserted my planned circuit and fled to the banks of green willows along the Charles River Esplanade to watch the ducks and attempt to gain a little perspective.

Down on the shores of the river I found a number of local wild plants struggling up from the moist soils: tick trefoil, smartweed, amaranth, and goosefoot, or chenopodium, a plant that was used by the native people of these parts for thousands of years. I knew from archeological records in the region that chenopodium was a common food source for the Indians; the seeds were discovered in abundance in archeological digs of temporary settlements, some of which were 8,000 years old. Also growing along the riverbank I noticed purple aster, seaside goldenrod, and, in the shallows, a healthy stand of cattails, whose beauty was unfortunately marred by the presence of water bottles, plastic bags, a condom, and a dead duck. Bankside litter notwithstanding, the river is relatively clean in our time and supports populations of smallmouth and largemouth bass, carp and perch and pike, migratory alewives and blue-backed herring.

I went out on the boat dock and sat cross-legged in the sun for a while looking upriver toward the modern city, most of which was built on land that did not exist in Katherine Nanny Naylor's time. In the foreground I could see the sculpted embankments, greensward, and park trees of the Esplanade, the blue waters of the Charles on my right, and beyond it the nation of Cambridge, another country in some ways, lower, more spired, bricked, and for the most part spared the glass towers of the modern city on my left. Dead ahead I could see the civilized brownstone walls of the Back Bay neighborhood, and farther off, poking up above the autumnal canopy, where the warblers were no doubt still foraging, the high towers of the new city: the prominence of the John Hancock Tower on the left, the garish fantastical Wizard of Oz–like tower known locally as the R2-D2 Building, and next to it the Prudential.

On this morning the river was empty of traffic save for a few sculls slipping by, a little flight of white butterflies in the form of the sailing school's sloops, and a kayak or two streaming along. I leaned back on my elbows and attempted to throw myself back into those earlier eras when the rivers and streams of the Northeast were undammed and clear and served as communal meeting grounds for normally warring tribes of local Indians at those times of year when migratory fish such as alewife and tom cod crowded together at narrows and falls. I thought then, as I have many times in the past, that Boston is an unreal city, a mere illusion that rises on this glacier-battered coast with false self-assurance, as if it were the hub of a great wheel and permanent in its centrality. I knew enough of geology by then to know that all is flux and that the land is as shifting and fluid as a wisp of morning mist.

I used to know a Native American from this area who claimed to have Massachusett tribal blood who shared this view, although for different reasons. When I first settled near Boston I was part of a study group that met once a month to discuss the fate of the waters of the Charles River and Boston Harbor. As far as I could tell, the group was a collection of older men who liked to get together to smoke cigars and reminisce about the old days around the harbor and the waterfront. One June day I came out from a particularly boring session and saw a man with long black hair in a ponytail, wearing what appeared to be snakeskin boots and a lot of silver and turquoise jewelry. For reasons I have never determined, he caught my eye, lifted his head, and greeted me—a rather odd greeting in fact.

"Been hunting?" he asked.

This took me aback. It was not hunting season, and I've never hunted in my life, but he looked familiar—I had known a couple of similar types from my past—so I stood talking with him for a while, trying to calculate where I might have met him. At the time I was involved in a research project concerning Indians during the Contact period, when the Europeans first landed on these shores, and since this man appeared to be Native American, or imagined himself to be, I engaged him in conversation.

He told me first that he was Mohawk, and when I expressed an interest in the fate of the Massachusett people, he told me his grandmother was part Massachusett and part Wampanoag, an extant tribe from Cape Cod.

The harbor preservation meetings were always held in an upstairs back room at the New England Aquarium, and to clear my head of cigar smoke and get some fresh air, I would walk along the harbor after I was freed. I saw my Indian friend there on several subsequent occasions. He said he was associated with tour groups to the restored version of the Pilgrims' Plimoth Plantation, which accounted for his presence along the harbor—not an entirely illogical explanation. Over that summer and fall I got to know him, and we would sometimes go over to a little pub he knew and share a glass or two.

He said his name was Thomas Blackfish, and he had recently returned to his home state after a long sojourn on the West Coast. He was a great ambitious liar as far as I could tell, who told me with apparently genuine sincerity about the oneness of the native people with their mother, the Earth, and how you must give back to the land whatever you take, and you must think how every action will affect those who are yet to come, even unto the seventh generation. Not bad advice, I suppose, but I had heard all this before from other native people and also—and mostly—from white members of what the Indians call the Wannabe Tribe. I liked Mr. Thomas Blackfish, though; I liked his easygoing, almost indifferent delivery of these beliefs. He had been down on his luck in life, he said, without being specific—probably undone by drugs—but whoever he was he seemed to have saved himself by his Indianness. I liked some of his theories, particularly those having to do with the sad decline of Boston. "What the hell, man," he told me at one point, "this was our land once. Now look at it."

Mr. Blackfish maintained a certain complacent attitude whenever I complained about the city and the local environment. He would tell me often that the European presence in "his" place was just temporary; the Indian time would come again.

"All these cars and trucks." he said. "That can't last. These high-rises. People living like birds on a cliff. You can't go on living like that for very long. It's going to end. And my people, they're still around. We'll be back."

All that was twenty-five years ago, and so far there have

been no signs of a total collapse of the city. But I suppose there will be time.

If I were to follow the metaphor of the hero's quest on this little walk, I would have crossed the Dark River at this point and made my way over to the mythic Isle of the Dead, the famed Mount Auburn Cemetery in Cambridge. This oasis, established in 1831, the first landscaped cemetery in the United States, has aged well and has become a veritable mecca for bird watchers, especially during migratory seasons. But on this particular trek I was attempting to concern myself with the Shawmut, and I still had a long way to go. In fact, I had hardly begun.

The Charles River, coupled with the Mystic to the north and the Neponset to the south, is another aspect of the geography of this place that drew the Europeans. The Pilgrims first landed on Cape Cod, coasted the shores of Cape Cod Bay, and, without exploring farther, settled in a little cove with a freshwater stream and named their town Plymouth. There they constructed permanent shelters and planted their fields. It was only on a later expedition up the coast that they came to a deep-water harbor, where they realized they should have settled in the first place.

On the west side lay an isolated peninsula topped with hills perfectly suited for fortification. To the north and south, three navigable rivers ran down to a deep-water harbor with many small islands. The Pilgrims considered uprooting and moving their whole settlement north, but decided it was too late; they were already dug in.

The Charles River, one of the defining aspects of Boston, snakes eastward to the coast from the low hills some twenty-five miles inland, in what is today the town of Hopkinton. It's a winding little river that runs for about eighty miles to get to the sea, fed along the way by some eighty small brooks and streams. Until it was dammed in certain sections along its route, the river provided some excellent sites for fish runs, hard-running narrows and falls where anadromous fish, which live in the open ocean and swim upstream each spring to breed, would crowd together.

The same was true of the Neponset to the south, which was even deeper and had in its headwaters a twelve-mile stretch of steep-sloped banks and many narrows where fish could be netted. Sections of both the Charles and the Neponset later became mill sites, their dams effectively cutting off the run of fish such as alewife and shad and salmon. In 1619 English traders based on Thompson Island in Boston Harbor set up a trading post on the banks of the Neponset, and by the 1630s, after the Puritans arrived, Richard Collicutt constructed a wharf on one of the river's tributaries to collect furs from the local Indians.

North of the city, the river the Indians called MissiTuk or "great tidal river"—today's Mystic River—cuts down to the harbor at an angle to the Charles. It flows out of the higher escarpment to the north, the Middlesex Fells, and the Lower Mystic Lake in Arlington, crossing or halting at many small lakes and ponds along its route, and then joins the Charles in what is today East Boston. East of the Mystic, the Saugus River also flows toward the harbor from the wall of the Fells and enters a band of extensive marshes along the coast.

The Indians commonly trapped fish in weirs, which consisted of stakes driven into the river bottom and interlaced with wattles. Migrating schools would be guided along the staked fence into the mouth of the weir, where they would be trapped and later netted in baskets, generally by women. Remnants of these fish weirs were discovered in the early twentieth century at three different sites during excavations for new buildings around Copley Square. Workers on the projects uncovered a network of upright posts driven into the mud some forty feet below the surface of the Back Bay in 1913. Archeologists determined that the posts were part of a massive system of weirs; all told, more than 65,000 stakes were found, as well as some of the intertwining wattles. When the stakes were dated, they turned out to be at least 5,000 years old, cut from local trees such as oak, birch, beech, and maple. The wattles were made of brushwood from the same species. The find, known as the Boylston Street Fish Weir, is still one of the most important and best documented of various prehistoric weirs that have been discovered along the East Coast. Originally the construction was believed to be a single very large weir, but later studies indicated that it was in fact a series of smaller weirs that had accumulated over time.

These discoveries, along with extensive shell middens found on the islands in the harbor, evidence of an ancient native foot trail on the Neck leading out to the Shawmut Peninsula, and various artifacts turned up during the Big Dig, indicate that this region was actively used by the Indians over a very long period of time.

The condition of the three Boston rivers is now much improved since the dark days of the mid-nineteenth-century industrial revolution, when they were befouled and clogged and downright dangerous to live beside. For all the city's celestial ambitions, environmental conditions began to decline in the decades following English settlement. Laws governing the treatment of land and waters did not exist in the time of John Winthrop, and by the middle of the nineteenth century this indifferent attitude toward the local environment had taken its toll. This was evident on land as well as in the surrounding waters. Privies were everywhere in the early decades of the city's existence, garbage was thrown out to wandering pigs, cows overgrazed the Common, and horses lay dead in the streets from time to time, giving off a stench that would infect whole neighborhoods. Dead dogs and cats, offal, and other "stinkeing things" lay rotting in the Common until, starting in the late 1600s, the city fathers finally saw fit to pass laws requiring that such offensive materials be buried.

In 1640 the city fathers constructed a milldam across a small cove between the North End and the main body of the peninsula. The mill, powered by the tides, worked well enough, but over the years the pond itself became a fetid, stinking cesspool. The locals threw dead animals and other foul matter into its waters. Drainage from privies and storm water ran down the slopes, making the pond so odoriferous and that section of the city so revolting that the city proprietors decided to act. "Out of sight, out of mind" was then a functioning form of environmental control, and the proprietors, following standard practice, filled the pond. In 1804 nearby Beacon Hill and Copp's Hill were stripped of their summits to provide the fill, and eventually the pond became part of Boston's made land, which now comprises most of the official city upland, from the Charles River on the north, around to the waterfront, the South End, and northwest to the Back Bay. Never mind that by the mid-twentieth century the area where the millpond was located had become as noisome as it was in the beginning, a wasteland of exhaust, litter, and ill-designed buildings, with little or no suggestion of organic life save for the occasional pedestrian who hurries along, collar turned up against the unrelenting winds of winter.

Sufficiently calmed by the quiet waters of the Charles, I resumed my journey. A little farther along the banks of the river, I came upon a company of women setting out sandwiches on makeshift tables. These were, I learned, volunteers from the Church of the Covenant, which runs a shelter for homeless women, and it seems that this was the day of their annual picnic. And a fine day it was, with the sparkle of sun on the nearby Charles and gulls circling overhead, a flotilla of swans out on the water, Canada geese rising and settling toward the Cambridge shore, and the whole of it overwashed with a healthy American blue. But clear skies, seemingly clean streets, the high glass towers of the burgeoning Boston economies, and the tree-lined river notwithstanding, the city has not yet achieved John Winthrop's model of the ideal city toward which the world would look as model. Not everyone in this city has achieved solvency. Even before the lunch was ready, a few early arrivals from the homeless shelters and the nearby mean streets appeared for the picnic and began accepting coffee, which the staff of the church also graciously shared with me.

The women did not appear to be an especially down-and-out lot, although a few seemed weathered from too many nights in the open air. Some had merely made a few bad choices and could no longer afford housing. Not an uncommon story. In my periodic rambles around this town, and with my propensity to fall into conversation with people whom the general public tends to avoid, I had heard it all before. Rising rents, overdue mortgage payments, drink, drugs, loss of employment, and in some cases bouts of mental illness had left these people without shelter.

I chatted with the women for a while and explained, in the course of conversation, my mission on this little walkabout. This begat, as I hoped it would, a number of stories of their own various nature encounters. The best came from a woman named Kathy, who, after spending a night in a church in Brookline, had emerged in the predawn hours onto a back street.

"It was a misty morning," she began. "There wasn't anybody around. No traffic, and I'm just wandering the streets there, under the trees and those big houses they have, and I see this cow coming down the middle of the road. Out of nowhere."

A friend of hers, an older, perhaps wiser, African American woman swathed in shawls and a headdress, gave her a cynical look, as if suggesting that Kathy had had too much to drink the night before.

"I mean it. This was real," Kathy said. "A cow. A black-and-white cow like you see on milk cartons."

I was tempted to tell her that, in theory at least, according to laws not yet excised from legal documents, the residents of Beacon Hill still have the right to keep cows in the city. I might also have mentioned that each June Boston still celebrates Dairy Day, when cows are returned to the Common to graze.

Her cow account gave rise to another story from Brookline. One afternoon, this woman said, she heard a cell phone ringing out from a dense thicket of shrubbery. She went to investigate and saw a bird fly off, but no cell phone.

I asked what the bird looked like.

"Gray," she said. "Big long tail, like."

"Mockingbird," I told her.

"You know birds?" the cynical African American woman asked me.

I said I did and took the opportunity to explain in more depth my mission that day.

I received in turn the same skeptical, disbelieving nod. No doubt she had lived long enough in the world to have seen all types and heard all the stories.

Southward then and back into the frantic streets, over Storrow Drive, up past the Hampshire House, and on into the sanctuary of the Public Garden.

There were many kitchen gardens on the peninsula after European settlement, but the frivolity of flowers, such as those that now grow in the Public Garden, as well as ornamental trees with no pragmatic use whatsoever, would have been anathema to the Puritans. This was, after all, a culture in which you could be fined for wearing fancy lace or silk. However, the Puritans were up against a generally unforgiving environment. When they first arrived they lived in "English wigwams," constructed by bending saplings together and covering the frame with skins or canvas. Later they built squalid little wattle-and-daub huts, clustered around the docks on the North End. They maintained grazing land, mostly on the Common, they fished, and they subsisted on a diet partly borrowed from the local

Indians, who lived on corn, beans, and squash, supplemented with wild game, shellfish, and wild plant foods such as berries and groundnuts, a tuberous plant not unlike large peanuts.

In subsequent years, matters did not proceed as John Winthrop and company had hoped. Among the Separatists, as the Pilgrims were called, even as early as 1620 in Plymouth, there were people of the Anglican persuasion and, worse, those with very little religion. These colonists were known as "Strangers," and in the early years, inasmuch as literal manpower was much in demand, they were tolerated. After 1630, during the Great Migration, more and more people of other sects, such as Baptists and Lutherans and the dreaded Quakers, began arriving on New England's shores, and these too the Puritans were forced to tolerate. Catholics, Jews, and infidels (read Indians—even converted Indians) were not tolerated, however. They were prohibited from settling on the peninsula and could not join the church, although, interestingly, the Puritans allowed Africans to join their congregations and live in the town.

But the renegade sects were on the rise, and in time the Puritans were forced to moderate their stance toward the "strangers." By the late 1600s the bonds of the church were loosened—slightly. None of this came easily. Some of the Puritans' most fanatical writings, such as the wonderful screeds by Cotton Mather concerning the presence of the Devil in New England, appeared at this time, just as the established order was weakening. Some historians suggest that the infamous witch trials of the period were a reaction to the perceived threats from outside the Puritan church.

Cotton Mather, from the third generation of American-born Mathers, was a brilliant student and preacher and, like his father, a leader in the theocracy that was Puritan Boston. His father, Increase Mather, was born in Dorchester in 1639, the son of the Reverend Richard Mather, who founded this powerful religious dynasty. Increase was appointed president of Harvard in 1692 and was active in politics, which in those times was not very far removed from religion. He was often away from the colony and back in England because of his political involvements. Connections with the homeland were beginning to weaken at this time, mainly because James II had revoked the Charter of Massachusetts and appointed Edmund Andros as governor of the newly created but short-lived Dominion of New England. Andros was no friend to Puritanism, and as a result of his haughty supervision the tentacles of the Anglican church were feeling their way toward the Puritan colony. Even the old Puritan bastion of South Church was temporarily appropriated for Anglican services at this time.

Increase Mather's son Cotton was also a preacher involved in politics and, also like his father, was associated with the Salem witch trials of 1692. Both father and son supported the use of spectral evidence, meaning that the fantastic dreams and even the visions of accusers could be admitted as evidence in the trials. But along with his interest in the mysteries of the unseen world, Cotton was also something of an early scientist and naturalist. He experimented with the hybridization of corn by observing the wind-borne pollination of red and blue corn by yellow corn. He also seems to have concerned himself with the observation of new species. At one point he got word of a beast known as an amphibaena in Newbury and made the arduous journey overland to see it. The amphibaena was an animal out of the medieval bestiaries, a two-headed snake that could travel in either direction and deliver a double sting. Given the other fantastical beings that spirited through the forests of Cotton's imagination, perhaps it was not such a rare entity. Suffice to say that he was unable to locate the beast.

But of all Cotton Mather's scientific involvements, none was more controversial than his use of inoculation against smallpox. He had learned from an African slave named Onesimus about a primitive form of inoculation used back in Africa and decided to test it. Cotton encouraged a local doctor to inoculate his own son as well as two slaves, an adult and a child. All three survived the experiment and were immune to the disease. But Cotton's experiment raised a storm of opposition. The doctor, Zabdiel Boylston, carried on with the practice in spite of death threats, later published the results of his experiments, and was subsequently elected to the Royal Society in London.

In his later years, Cotton Mather began to question his own beliefs about the use of spectral evidence and eventually rejected it. At the same time, he seems to have softened his attitude toward wild nature. In fact, in certain ways his views predated some of the thinking of the Concord transcendentalists. He began to see the natural world as the temple of God, the "Almighty Architect." He cited nature as a "Publick Library," prefiguring in some ways the Romantic era—Wordsworth's "sermons in stones" and the like. There is even a little of the mystic William Blake in his writings. Cotton had access to the newly invented microscope and was able to observe the real wonders of the unseen world; he wrote enthusiastically about the marvel of seeds and fruits and the fact that a particle no larger than a grain of sand could produce the "astonishing elegancy" of a plant. He even anticipated Thoreau's now famous work "The Dispersal of Seeds," marveling at the myriad ways in which plants manage to scatter and sow their seeds. Cotton Mather continued to hold fast to the Judeo-Christian metaphor of sin as a wilderness, however, a place full of doleful creatures, with wild beasts crying in its desolate houses and dragons in its most pleasant palaces. Nevertheless, partly through his work, an alternative view of nature had been launched.

I was skirting both time and topography by crossing the Public Garden. In 1630 I probably would have been slogging through wetlands at this point on my circuit. But by the 1850s, the natural world had been turned upside down, and on a twenty-five-acre section of landfill at the southwest end of the Common, amateur horticulturalists banded together and commissioned a local architect, George Meacham, to lay out a garden open to the public.

This section, among schoolchildren at least, is perhaps the best-known site in the city, inasmuch at it is the location of the Lagoon and the Swan Boats, and the destination of Mr. and Mrs. Mallard and their ducklings, who in Robert McCloskey's perennial classic *Make Way for Ducklings* became disoriented and had to make their way through traffic to their home on the Lagoon. There is, to this day, no lack of real mallard ducks in the Lagoon. But back in 1987, the city commissioned the sculptor Nancy Schön to recreate the family in bronze, and the sculpted ducks now seem to attract more children than the real ones. Their heads and backs are worn to a golden gloss by the myriad hands of young admirers.

Spring, when the Kwanzan cherries and the tulips and daffodils and azaleas are all abloom, is probably the best time to wander through the Public Garden. But in any season, other than perhaps the dead of winter, it has its charms. Now, in September, the summer annuals were still in flower, although a gardener I met named Kevin was uprooting the fading zinnias and cosmos in spite of the fact that we were a long way from the first frost. I could not help but be impressed with the quality of the soil in this section of the city. It was rich, dark, and crumbly, having been lovingly supplemented for more than one hundred years. In an as yet unturned section of the flower bed, I also noticed what I believed to be an oyster mushroom, a species more commonly found in local forests at this time of year.

Kevin, a tall, sandy-haired man, at first seemed a little leery about sharing information with a wandering stranger such as myself who, without introduction, arrived and began to ask specific questions about zinnias and the decidedly exotic tropical plants that were also growing in the plots he was uprooting. His answers were noncommittal. "That's right," for example. "You got it." "Yup." But in time he warmed up and began to answer some of my questions and soon was spouting off with pride about the Garden.

He explained that there were something like eighty different varieties of flowers and shrubs, as well as more than one hundred different species of trees, including a few ornamental rarities such as a Camperdown elm and a weeping pagoda tree.

"We've got a lot of different cherries here," he said, "and lindens, beeches, a Kentucky coffee tree, a sequoia, and even palms."

I questioned this. Palms, of course, are subtropical, and

global warming notwithstanding, surely were unable to survive a Boston winter.

"We dig them up and move them to the greenhouses at the Arnold Arboretum each autumn," Kevin said.

He explained that the palms and some of the garish (in my view) coleuses and cockscombs are newer additions to the annual beds, an attempt to recreate the original plants of the Victorian garden that was first laid out here in the 1850s.

Even though he was apparently a hired man sent out to clean the flower beds for the coming season, Kevin seemed to know a great deal about plants and the gardens. He explained that in winter he was the director of some office at the Arboretum, in Jamaica Plain.

"Look me up if you're over that way," he said.

I said I would and bade farewell. But, interestingly enough, some months later, doing a little homework at the Arboretum, I tried to find him. No one there had ever heard of him.

The Public Garden is now certainly the most floriferous part of the peninsula, and given the fact that it harbors any number of exotic species, probably offers more diversity of plant life than the peninsula has ever been able to maintain. Boston is, after all, a cold, exposed jut of land on the rock-hard northeastern coast of North America.

In point of fact, the place where the two of us stood chatting was once a stinking fen, the end point for the accumulated sewage and tides of the Charles River flats. The Public Garden emerged as high ground only after a great deal of political maneuvering. The site, originally known as Round Marsh, was a pristine little cove and a popular fishing and clamming area until the increasing population of the city polluted it. Then, following the custom of this town, to solve the problem they covered it up. At least in the case of Round Marsh they saw fit to put in a garden rather than some noxious commercial development.

In 1630 the tidal marsh at this site presumably nurtured most of the species that can still be found in the marshes of the salt rivers of Massachusetts in our time: rushes and reeds, native grasses such as red and black spartina and cord grass, and also, according to the archeological records, a native phragmites. Herein were killifish, the young of offshore fish species, hermit crabs, green crabs, horseshoe crabs, ribbed mussels, and periwinkles, as well as higher species such as muskrats, raccoons, red-winged blackbirds, rails, bitterns, egrets, herons, and dabbling ducks.

Now protected by law—in theory at least—salt marshes, which once surrounded the riverbanks and bay shores of Boston, are among the most productive ecosystems on earth. They harbor a rich diversity of life, much of it microscopic, and serve as nurseries and nutrient sources for the predators and prey that make up the great food pyramids of marine life farther offshore. Most of the salt marshes are gone now, having been filled to make way for the modern city long before there were laws governing such actions. But across the river in East Boston, one of the last of the region's salt marshes, Belle Isle Marsh, which is maintained by the Massachusetts Department of Conservation and Recreation, preserves 152 acres of this critical habitat. Many plants and animals that are now rare in the greater metropolitan area still thrive here. Like Mount Auburn Cemetery, the marsh has become a local bird-watching area. Bitterns and black-crowned night herons, ducks and dowitchers, glossy ibis, oystercatchers, and other birds that city-bound bird watchers used to travel long distances to find either nest or pass through the marsh during migratory seasons.

Beyond the Public Garden I came upon a warren of urban canyons, traffic, side streets, crowds, and more exhaust, not the most pleasant atmosphere for this September day. Elsewhere within the city limits meadow crickets were singing in the sunlight, asters and goldenrods were flowering, and little flights of Savannah sparrows were passing through the weedy edges of the community gardens over on the Fenway. But the so-called theater district, on the southeast side of the Common, does not have the occasional havens of respite that can be found on the northern and western sides of the peninsula. This section, along with the North End, was in fact an area of early settlement. Old maps of Boston show a density of streets and docks and warehouses here even in the seventeenth century, whereas the Common and the northern side of Beacon Hill were relatively undeveloped and supported orchards and vegetable plots.

Nonetheless, in order to stay true to the course of my pilgrimage, I forged on, past lifeless walls dripping with grime, then turned onto Tremont Street and headed down toward Shawmut Avenue—a rather ill-named street, given the original nature of the peninsula, with its frog-loud hollows and forested hills and shady glades.

Soon I came upon a veritable tidal bore of traffic and exhaust in the form of the Massachusetts Turnpike, which I skirted, passing along Marginal Road to Washington Street, where I encountered a conglomeration of contemporary Americana so vast as to cause John Winthrop and Samuel Sewall and old Increase Mather to fall into apoplexy could they view the brash lights and commercialism that has overcome their ideal city. But onward, up Washington Street through the maelstrom until I reached another ill-named byway, Oak Street.

There are still oak trees on the Shawmut Peninsula, but they were planted later, beginning in the nineteenth century. I could not find a single oak on Oak Street, nor on Oak Place, where I turned left and headed north. And no ash trees, for that matter, on Ash Street, and no sand on Beach Street, which I passed later.

It is curious that it was not until the 1650s, twenty years after the Puritans settled in this place, that the city fathers took it upon themselves to actually give names to the streets they had created. Before that the paths and tracks were called by what they were—"the path to the harbor," for example, or "the great highway to Roxberre." All these twists and turns and dead ends and cul-de-sacs were not laid out by wandering cows, as is often claimed in the tourist guidebooks. They were, as is fitting for so human a city, the pathways of the English inhabitants themselves, and one was an old Indian trail along the Neck, which followed what is now the sadly debased Washington Street.

Nonmaterialistic ideals of the Puritan theocracy notwithstanding, the die was cast for these worldly developments in Boston early on in the English settlement. The crass commercialism of Washington Street, repulsive though it would have been to the Puritans, probably would please the Massachusett Indians, were they with us now. They and the tribes to the south and north, the Narrangansetts, Pokanokets, and Missi-Tucs were mad for English goods, especially guns, knives, and axes, but also beads and baubles and decorative clothes—the brighter the better. One account I know of describes a ceremony around 1675 in which Queen Weetamoo, a *saunk,* or female head of a clan or tribe, appeared at a dance in full regalia. Wearing her usual shell and feather ornaments, she had powdered her face white and wore English skirts, with chains of beads and high, spangled boots.

More worldly Anglicans and other "strangers" were living in the town in the decades after settlement. And even before Boston was settled, just to the south, in what is now Quincy, there came into the country a man who was an abomination to both the Puritans of Boston and the Pilgrims of Plymouth.

Thomas Morton was of a different class from the hard-working Pilgrims and Puritans. Born of an Anglican family, he appears to have been an irreligious sort, a veritable "lord of Misrule," as he was characterized by the Pilgrim governor William Bradford. Morton and a company of merry men set up a trading post at what he called Merrymount and immediately began trading goods with the Indians. Unlike the Pilgrims, whom he seems to have disdained, Morton soon fell into the local Indian customs, hunting and fishing, gambling and sporting with the local natives, and living well off the land, while his poor countrymen to the south at Plymouth were on the verge of starvation.

The Indians took a liking to Morton and his company of men, and soon he was garnering more furs for trade than were the Pilgrims or the Puritans. His fellow Englishmen were appalled by his behavior and more than once clapped him in irons.

In fact on one occasion he was bound up in a hideous device know as the bilbo, an iron bar that shackled the transgressor's legs and hands and chained him to an upright post.

Morton's greatest sin seems to have been his heathenish ways and the high life he was leading among the Indians—who were as fond of bright fripperies, dancing, and gambling as he and his men were. According to Bradford, Morton maintained at Merrymount a "school of Atheism," where he quaffed wine and strong waters with his Indian friends. What was especially offensive, apparently, was that he set up a paganistic Maypole and began drinking and dancing with the local Indian maidens, "frisking together (like so many fairies, or furies rather) . . . and worse practices," as Bradford wrote. At one point, Morton's happy few, unburdened in the freedom of the wilds, organized a feast in honor of the Roman goddess Flora, Bradford claimed, and reenacted the beastly practices of the mad Bacchanalians. Morton compounded the problem by composing sundry off-color verses and rhymes and songs, mocking his fellow English. He referred to Miles Standish, who was small of stature, as "ye Captain Shrimp," among other things.

It was all too much for the Puritans and the Pilgrims. They sent Captain Shrimp and a company of men to arrest Morton and his merry pranksters. Fortunately for the Pilgrim soldiers, most of Morton's people were drunk when Standish arrived, and Morton was captured without a skirmish. He was carried away to Plymouth, where he was kept in chains until a ship came from the Isle of Shoals and took him back to England.

After his banishment to his native land, Morton wrote a tract, *The Manner and Customs of the Indians of New England*, which was a detailed, almost anthropological, account of Native American spiritual beliefs, hunting practices, sorcery, food, and shelters. It was a sympathetic portrait and hardly characterized the Indians as barbarous heathens. He dispassionately recorded the practices of their religion without judgment.

There is an alternative account of the land in which these early English settlers were living, as well as a few incidental glimpses of the Native American way of life, in Governor William Bradford's *History of Plymouth Plantation.* Bradford offers what is certainly one of the coldest descriptions of the world that the struggling Pilgrims were up against when they landed on these shores after a grueling four-month crossing of the North Atlantic.

> *And as for the season it was winter, and they that know the winters of that countrie know them to be sharp and violent and subjecte to cruell and fierce stormes... beside what could they see but a hidious and desolate wilderness, full of wild beasts and wild men... For summer being done, all things stand upon them with a weatherbeaten face, and the whole countrie, full of woods and thickets, represented a wild and savage heiw.*

Compare that with the favorable notes from Morton and John Smith and a few others who coasted along these shores, and the question arises of the actual nature of the land they were invading. Was it a desolate wilderness, or was it the Paradise of all these parts?

Wilderness as an inhuman place separated from and alien to the human experience, filled with wild beasts and savages, is basically a Western construct. The idea of a separation between the settled world and the wild world did not really occur to the native tribes in this region. Night may have seemed dangerous, filled with imaginary gods and monsters, and the local Indians never did venture up to mountaintops, since these were known to be the realm of dangerous gods and spirits. But the forests and even deep swamps and fens were considered benign, sources of food and refuge, closer in some ways to the European concept of a garden.

By contrast, for the Europeans, and most especially for the orderly Puritans and Pilgrims, wilderness was a dangerous place, beyond human control and threatening in both physical and metaphysical ways. Out in the dark forests beyond the Shawmut Peninsula lay the savage world, where anything could go wrong. There were in fact wild beasts—bears and wolves and catamounts—living on the mainland, although how dangerous they were is open to question. But more to the point in the English mind, apart from these apparent physical dangers, in the primitive, otherworldly wild forest you could easily lose direction, become "bewildered," and revert to the prelapsarian godlessness of the Indians. That was perhaps the greater danger. Here, in the dark forests of the Puritan imagination, according to Cotton Mather, the fiery worm flew by night, bewitched madwomen danced around devil fires, and errant veiled ministers, priests, and papists, imps, serpents, cats, owls, and fiends of all manner cavorted in the firelight and engaged in unspeakable rituals and communions with unseen black entities.

Two hundred years later, Nathaniel Hawthorne caught the spirit of the times in his account of the adventures of young Goodman Brown, who strayed into such a coven of devils and himself became bewitched.

In our time we have to deal metaphorically with another sort of wilderness, the so-called jungle of the streets. Near the streets along which I was walking on this fall day lay Boston's former Combat Zone, a section of the city devoted to strip joints, prostitution, and street crime that took over from an equally degenerate zone known as Scollay Square, which was cleared in the 1960s to make way for the ambitious and lifeless stone desert known as Government Center. In its heyday the Combat Zone was bad enough to be cited in Boston guidebooks as a place to be avoided by night, although visitors to the city went there anyway, as they had to Scollay Square before it. Now, like Times Square in New York, the Combat Zone is gone, its loss hardly lamented by the local Chinese families who live close by.

For my part, I passed along Washington Street, with all its materialistic temptations and defunct strip joints, untempted by worldly goods. Born of Anglican parents, and having strayed into a debased heathenism in my adult years, I nonetheless bear within me a dying ember of the old Puritan ethic; I was as repulsed by the cheap treasures of this earth on Washington Street as the old witch hunter Cotton Mather would have been. I cleared the area as soon as I could, turned onto Essex Street, and made my way toward the former shoreline near South Station, an area that in John Winthrop's time probably was flooded twice a day by the rising tides of the harbor.

This was a particularly windy section of the coast in 1630, open to the dreaded east winds of the North Atlantic, which have a fairly long fetch at this point. Never ones to avoid use of an available resource, early on the city fathers erected a series of windmills in this area, once known as Windmill Point, to grind their grain. Now it's an unremarkable section of windy city streets where errant birds of paper and plastic litter swirl in the gritty airs.

Local winds are the bane of commuters in our time. In winter, those making their way to the offices of the financial district are battered and torn and chilled by the sea winds, which are increased and channeled by the high-rise cliffs of the city buildings. Even in summer the winds, which are generally out of the southwest in this season, pick up litter and dust and sting the eyes on certain days.

The role of these local winds is often overlooked in historical accounts of Boston. Along with the harbor and the sea and the bitterly chill winters, wind is very much a part of the character of this nautical city. In any season but summer, northeasters come driving down across the North Atlantic and hammer the city for two or three days at a time, wrecking ships in former days, downing wires and trees and even killing people in our time. Aside from this ill wind from the northeast, the west and south winds, benevolent and predictable, provided the power for the local coastal trade. Ultimately those winds carried local ships around the world and turned Boston into one of the most important seaports in the United States in the first two centuries of its existence.

Wind was also, in some oblique ways, part of my own introduction to this port city. I grew up in a household that upheld the clipper ship as some sort of sacred icon and the shipbuilder Donald McKay as an earthly version of the archangel. I was the youngest by many years in a family of five and barely understood what all this meant, but I understood that clipper ships were ranked somewhere between heaven and earth, that they were fast, that they sailed the seven seas, and that they emanated from a place called Boston, to which, from time to time, they came home to roost.

Periodically, my father would take down from the shelf the veritable bible of these matters, Samuel Eliot Morison's *Maritime History of Massachusetts,* and read aloud, as from sacred texts, the description of the arrival of a clipper ship in Boston Harbor after a voyage around the world:

> *A summer day with the scent of new cut hay on the salt air, a clipper ship in the offing, slowly emerging from Massachusetts Bay with all sails set, sailing past Boston Light, hauling a few points on the wind to shoot the Narrows between Georges, Gallups, and Lovells Islands, and then paying off again through President Road, and finally booming up the stream past the Castle, where lounging soldiers, out for a breath of sea air, would be struck dumb with wonder at the beauty of it all.*

My father would close the book solemnly at this point and there would be a devout silence around the table. Over the mantel we had an oil painting of Donald McKay's ship *Flying Cloud* running before the wind—all sails set, of course. I seem to remember my father bowing toward it after the reading. But that is probably faulty memory.

Given this background, it is perhaps fitting that I first saw Boston from sea. I was working as a deck hand on a schooner that was making its way up the coast from New York to Maine, stopping at little ports here and there to take on supplies or shelter. Early one July morning, shortly after we passed through the Cape Cod Canal, I came out on deck and saw a brownish fog on the shoreline. Rising through the mists were the towers of the coastal city. Later, as the little vessel plowed along, the fog cleared and the morning sun caught the hilled skyline and the gray-brown granite of the buildings, their windows flashing in the burnished morning sun, all bright and looking for all the world like John Winthrop's divine city, save that the signature hills had been leveled. This was before the construction of what came to be called the "new Boston," and compared to high-rise New York, Boston had the appearance of a small European port city.

My first introduction to the actual streets of the city came at the age of eighteen or nineteen, when I was sent to Boston to find my older brother, who was living hand-to-mouth in the city with no real address, attempting to support himself as a maritime painter. I had a vague sense of where he was and some information from mutual friends to go by, and after some casting about and questioning of students in the general area, I found him. He was living for free in the attic of a brownstone on the corner of Fairfield Street and Commonwealth Avenue. At the time he was in the process of restoring a sleek-hulled 1946 powerboat he had renamed the *R. H. Dana,* which was pulled up in Esterhill's Boatyard on Chelsea Creek in East Boston—not the best address in town, it should be said.

I dutifully delivered his mail and the many messages from our parents and spent a few days in his attic.

Having grown up near New York City, I found Boston to be a benign and kindly environment in those bright years; the trees along Commonwealth Avenue offered a sheltering canopy over the green central walkway, the old French Empire–styled buildings were lined up one after another, some in a state of splendid decline, some well cared for, with polished brass doorknobs and freshly painted trim. Furthermore, the people of the city seemed to be younger and more angular than those in New York, and they moved along the streets with determination and direction, but without the frenzied, attack-dog velocity of New Yorkers. The green parks along the Charles were only a few blocks away, and I had to walk but a few blocks east to get to the Common.

I remember that on more than one occasion wild birds, which I now realize were chimney swifts, flew in and out of my brother's open windows, and I also remember some slim, long-winged birds that would spirit over the city rooftops at dusk. In retrospect, I realize they were nighthawks, birds in the same family as whip-poor-wills, which nest on the flat roofs of the city and feed on the rising clouds of midges and other insects between May and late August.

After that first introduction, I came to like the place, and since I had friends in colleges there, I would make regular pilgrimages from New York—which I hated—sometimes staying with my brother, sometimes with friends. All this was in the mid-1960s, an era, as I later learned, when, in the eyes of local urban watchers, Boston was in sad decline.

By this point in my trek I was beginning to get hungry, and I hurried along Atlantic Avenue with the intention of getting over to the North End for a good lunch. I turned up Oliver Street and began to weave through the rat maze of the financial district. Near here, at what is now International Place, a steep drumlin once rose some eighty feet above the current street level. In the 1630s this was the location of Corn Hill, one of the defining eminences of the Shawmut. By the time the Puritans arrived, the hill may have been cleared by the Massachusett people, or else the Puritans had harvested the timber early on, since this was the site of one of their first corn plantations. After several growing seasons, as access to the planting grounds beyond the Neck became available, the city officials built a fort on the site and changed the name to Fort Hill—which I believe says something about the condition of the world at that time.

Back in England in the 1630s, Charles I was having a little problem with the rising tides of Puritans and other Protestant groups that believed he was growing too close to Catholic Europe. Among other insults Charles had married a Catholic, Henrietta Maria. By 1641 the tensions had broken out into downright civil war, and after a series of ill-thought-out political maneuvers, Charles was arrested, tried, and beheaded. Oliver Cromwell took over as military dictator, and the eleven-year interregnum began. Catholicism was banished; Parliament was abolished, and theater and dancing and other frivolities were outlawed.

It was not a bad period for the Puritans of the American colonies. England had more local problems: the battles at Marston Moor, troublesome priests, the Irish Rebellion, and the subsequent sieges of Wexford and Drogheda. As a result the mother country more or less left the colonies alone, though around Boston, there were troubles on the high seas. French men-of-war periodically ranged along the coast, piracy was beginning to threaten local shipping, and to the south there was a little problem brewing with the Massachusett Indians at Wessagusett, in what is now Weymouth.

The Pilgrims had had to deal earlier with a few minor tensions with the Indians. Then at Wessagusett there was rumored to have been an alliance developing between the Narragansetts and the Massachusett people to attack Plymouth and get rid of these problematic English. Feisty little Miles Standish marched up to the Massachusett territory, killed one of the ringleaders, and abused and insulted other local Indian tribes, some of them tractable and formerly favoring the English. The threat was put down (or at least postponed—it would rise again in the form of King Philip's War in 1675), but tension between the English and the Indians increased.

On its easily defended peninsula, Boston was protected from the Indians, but threats from the sea still remained. In 1632 John Winthrop was forced to send out a naval expedition to attempt to capture a renegade pirate with the odd name of Dixie Bull, who had come over to Boston from London the year before to trade with the Indians. Bull had been attacked and robbed by a French ship and, as a result of the raid, turned to piracy to recoup his losses and began plaguing ships of all nations off the New England coast. He is credited with the honor of being New England's first pirate.

Nothing remains of this harsh but interesting past world in the plant-barren, lifeless environment I was walking through. Beyond the burrows of dark streets and exhaust, out in the suburbs and woodlands stretching west to Mount Wachusett, this September day must have ranked very high on the list of perfect autumn days, for which New England is famed. As it was, I had to be content with whatever small flowerings I could find in the empty lots and sidewalk cracks.

I determined to take my midday meal out of doors and, deserting my ambling walkabout, began to make my way to a place called Fiore in the North End, which I knew had an outdoor patio and even rooftop dining. I also knew from past experience that the chef there knew how to make gnocchi, not always the safest choice in an American-based Italian restaurant.

The North End, which is—or at least was—the Italian section of the city, still resembles small-town Italy in some ways. Italy had won the World Cup a few days before my little sojourn, and a replica of the cup was coming to Hanover Street to be admired—even worshipped—by the locals. The streets were full and closed to traffic for the event, and the police were hauling away the parked vehicles of outsiders, much to the amusement of the locals, I noticed.

Not to digress into cultural rather than natural history, but Boston is a sports-crazed city—yet another attribute of this modern town that no doubt would have deeply offended Increase Mather, John Winthrop, and company. Public sports were prohibited by law in Puritan Boston; you could do time in the pillory for lawn bowling. (The bowling ball that Katherine Nanny Naylor or her husband threw down their privy would have been used privately, maybe even secretly.)

I managed to secure a rooftop table above the fray of the streets, ordered a glass of Lacrima di Cristo wine, and settled back to wait for my gnocchi. Big jets were sailing in over the rooftops to Logan Airport, car horns beeped below in the streets, there were shouts in English, curses in Italian, the annoying warning bell of tow trucks hauling off cars, more jets, a deep-throated hoot from a freighter in the harbor, more shouts and clamor, and then, like a cloud above me, sweeping across the rooftops—a flight of starlings.

Rats, pigeons, and starlings are the most common forms of wildlife in some sections of this city. The rats, according to homeless people I know, are common denizens of the night, as common as squirrels, I was told. Pigeons are everywhere, and starlings roost in huge twittering flocks anywhere they can find enough trees. The Fenway is a favorite daytime territory, and thousands of starlings roost under the bridges where I-93 and Route 1 split, just north of the city. In fact, the great wheeling horde circling above me could have been part of this flock.

I'm not sure I could make an argument for rats, and save for a few lonely citizens who congregate in Boston's public parks each day to feed "their" birds, many people despise pigeons. But as far as I'm concerned, starlings are another matter. I do appreciate their hopeful chatter when they come in to roost, and I love the whistling of their spring song. But mostly I love to see the great flocks that band together in early autumn and stay together through the winter.

Years ago, when I was imprisoned on the island of Manhattan, amid the dark satanic conurbation of dead canyons and high winds, my one respite, other than the great green sanctuary of Central Park, was to walk over to the West Side and watch the clouds of starlings sweeping across the river in the purple winter twilight to roost on the cliff walls of the Palisades. They are beautiful birds when they're decked out in their spring plumage; caught in the proper raking light, their feathers display a veritable prism of colors, and their wheeling flocks add a touch of an old, perhaps more enduring, world for urban dwellers who live seemingly cut off from the rhythms of wild nature.

After lunch I headed over to the Copp's Hill Burying Ground to rest in the sun and sleep off my substantial midday meal. I worked through the madding crowd surging down Hanover Street to see the World Cup and then cut through the Prado, the tree-lined allée that leads to the Old North Church. Here, in the paving stones, were the fallen dried seeds of linden trees plus a few struggling dandelions and other weeds heartily pushing up through the flags. This admirable little park, reminiscent of so many small passageways in Europe, offered an excellent contrast to the busy streets beyond.

The little spit of land known as the North End is the most historic section of the city. It was here, close to the newly constructed wharfs, that the Puritans laid out their first dwellings. Contrary to popular history, which holds that the streets of Boston form an illogical maze, the Puritans built their new town more or less according to traditional European settlement patterns, a series of concentric streets and pathways flowing out from the docks. Later, in 1634, they raised the funds to purchase the Common from Blackstone, and over the next few decades the North End slowly expanded to the southwest. Even in among the crowded houses there were planting grounds, however. The Prado was once a pasture, and Copp's Hill, formerly known as Windmill Hill, which, like Corn Hill and Windmill Point, was the site of one of the earliest windmills in the town. It was a favored location, high above the harbor and the mouth of the Charles and situated in such a way that it caught both east and west winds.

Housing conditions in these early years were decidedly primitive. The substantial saltboxes and garrison houses of colonial New England would come later. Most of the early Puritan families crowded together in their English wigwams, which were essentially Native American structures. The more substantial of these dwellings had a framed doorway instead of a skin flap, and some of them had a stone or wattle fireplace at one end for cooking and heat, unlike the Indian shelters, which had a fire pit and a hole open to the sky and were often dense with cooking smoke. The Puritans covered their floors with rushes, and when the rushes became too infested with fleas and lice and food scraps, the flooring would be swept out and burned and replaced with fresh plant material. The Indians had a similar system, save that they would simply burn the whole wigwam and rebuild. Some English families on the peninsula burrowed into the ground and lived like moles in shelters dug into the hills of the Shawmut. Others dwelt in tents the first winter and no doubt shivered through the long nights.

All this was temporary, of course, until they could build more substantial English-style framed houses, which they thatched with local marsh grasses, probably the phragmites reeds that grew in abundance along the Charles River marshes and still grow along the Muddy River in the Fenway. Although it is now being crowded out by a more aggressive nonnative variety, phragmites is a native reed and was common in the 1630s. Archeologists turned up pollen remains of the plants associated with the Boylston Street Fish Weir used by the Indians 5,000 years ago.

The Puritans brought over some of their local architectural customs from rural England. Thatch-roofed dwellings were not uncommon in East Anglia, where most of the immigrants had come from, and wattle-and-daub housing, in which saplings were woven around a frame and then chinked with mud mixed with sand and vegetation, was still in use back in England. The big difference as far as construction materials were concerned was that America had extensive forests. Wood was at a premium in England in the seventeenth century, and one of the common praises of the New World sung by early travelers was of the abundance of trees for fuel and building. Also the profusion of wild game. It should be said that these early records bear a close reading. They were to some extent advertisements to encourage settlement—no one but Bradford makes much mention of the ferocity of the New England winter, for example.

But the forests of New England *were* extensive, although the dense thickets of shrubs that you see now did not exist throughout the region. In some sections, the understory had been burnt over by the Indians to encourage the growth of blueberries, an ingredient in the Indian trail food known as pemmican, which was a mix of bear fat, berries, and pulverized dried meat. The berries that grew in after the fires also provided food for the white-tailed deer, another staple of the Indian diet.

Although the early accounts of New England contained a few imaginary beasts such as the amphibaena, there must have been some truth to the tales of abundant game. Even in the late seventeenth century, the waters near the mouth of the Charles River would have been alive with striped bass, white perch, mackerel, cod, and sturgeon, one of which is on record as measuring eighteen feet in length and two feet between the eyes. The runs of anadromous fish such as alewives, shad, and even salmon were astonishing to the early settlers, so thick in some river narrows that it was said—no doubt erroneously—that you could cross a stream on their backs. In autumn there were eels, so-called catadromous fish, which live in fresh water and then swim down to the Sargasso Sea to breed. In spring millions of young eels, or elvers, would collect off the coasts to run up the local rivers and streams to the ponds where they would spend most of their lives. These too the Puritans must have trapped, since even now in England elvers are a traditional springtime dish.

Along with the fish were vast supplies of deer, bear, turkeys, passenger pigeons, woodcock, immense flocks of geese, ducks, and swans, and shore birds in both spring and autumn. There were also upland species such as snipe, woodcock, grouse, heath hens, and upland sandpipers. Later the English had their own beef and pork and mutton from animals they raised on the Common and in the open fields of the former Indian gardens out on the islands. The pigs would have been turned out into the forest to fend for themselves and then rounded up in autumn after they had fed on the mast crop. The English also fed upon a profusion of wild plant foods borrowed from the Indian traditions, such as groundnuts, blueberries, huckleberries, and grapes. Early on they brought over slips or seeds of apple trees, which they planted near Windmill Point.

William Blackstone had imported a bag of pips, or apple seeds, and planted an orchard on Beacon Hill consisting of a British variety known as Yellow Sweeting. How many of his trees bore fruit in his time is questionable, however, since there were no honeybees in the colony at first. Back in Suffolk, John Winthrop had been a farmer and orchardist before he came over, and he may have been the one responsible for the cultivation of the apple that came to be known as the Roxbury Russet, the first variety developed in North America. Winthrop later imported bees and even sent a hive and more pips down to Blackstone, who had by then settled in Rhode Island.

Apples were an important crop for the New World settlers. They were not planted for eating, however, but were used to make cider, one of the staple beverages, along with beer, of the Pilgrims and Puritans. It is telling that in an account of an expedition up the coast, Bradford reported—in exasperation—that the explorers ran out of beer and were forced to quench their thirst with water.

You would have thought that with this cornucopia of foodstuffs no one would have starved in this New World. And yet, especially in the early years, only that detested transgressor Thomas Morton seems to have appreciated the fact that to survive well one had but to go native, as the phrase has it, and live as the Indians did. Morton was an avid hunter and fisherman, and also a skilled trader, and he and his merry band seem to have had an almost perpetual Thanksgiving feast, only with more drinking and sporting, dancing, and "worse practices" with the local Indian maidens, as Bradford pointed out—and all this in spite of very few prayers of thanks. Later seventeenth-century reports of Indian life marvel at how the natives managed to find food even in the dead landscape of winter in New England.

Up on Copp's Hill I found a place in the sun and lay down on the grass with my head propped against a brick wall. I dozed off and half dreamed of the founders and inhabitants of this imaginative and, one might even say, brave experiment in an alien land. Here, inscribed in stone with their names and dates, was the evidence of their being—English and African alike, alone on a cold coastal peninsula, separated, as William Bradford wrote, from their former homes by the cold gulf of the Atlantic. Among other notables, Increase Mather and his fiery son, Cotton, are buried here. And along with the well-known Bostonians are the remains of the merchants and craftsmen and artisans of the old North End community. Here too were buried the African slaves and freemen who lived in the section of Boston near the North End known as New Guinea.

What is unfortunate, given the events that were to follow in the next 250 years, is that these otherwise courageous individuals did not learn more about living in balance with the local environment from the indigenous people whom they uprooted. The Puritans carried across the Atlantic their concept of a great chain of being, with a powerful male god at the top, angels below, below them God's own children, and within this suborder an elaborate church hierarchy of a chosen few pious clergymen, a congregation of male parishioners below them, with women at the lowest human level, and below them, the animals, then the plants, and below that and hardly recognized as an entity, the rocks and soils of the earth.

In a way, they had the system reversed. Their god should have been the sustaining soil; their saints and angels the plants and animals that supplied them with life. But they were prisoners of the seventeenth century, and very few had any concept of what we now term ecological systems. Even the supposedly ecologically sensitive Indians were not entirely without blame. Although they lived in a seemingly more benign relationship with their land—they thanked the deer and bears whom they slaughtered for giving themselves up, for example, and they understood the necessity of returning nutrients to the soil—they seem to have lacked a long-term ecological appreciation of their role in the world. New research suggests that the native people of the Americas (who were themselves immigrants) may have been responsible for the great Pleistocene overkill that drove the mastodons and mammoths and giant elks and stag-moose to extinction. Later, after the Indians began trading with the Europeans, they willingly wiped out the beaver and decimated the herds of white-tailed deer in exchange for European trade goods.

But then we modern residents too are trapped in our own limited view of the complex systems of nature. And even though we may have a slightly better idea of how things work in the natural world and what we should or should not do to protect our resources, we are certainly no better behaved than the Puritans, maybe a little worse, since we supposedly know what we are doing.

I woke up from my reveries in desperate need of coffee and walked back into the maelstrom of the modern world, with its cars and trucks and surging hordes of World Cup worshippers. Just outside the gate to the graveyard I saw two kerchiefed ladies sitting on a bench in front of their apartment, which overlooked the burying ground. I asked them if they ever saw any ghosts of the Puritan fathers hovering over the stones at night.

"Just one," they said. "And he's friendly. Never did nobody any harm."

A double espresso later, I was back working my way through the narrow maze courses leading to Commercial

Street, which runs along the site of the former dam that once held back the waters of the millpond. From here I passed through the architectural wasteland of Government Center, with its barren, windy open spaces, and made my way up the back side of Beacon Hill to the Common, where I had begun.

The evening rush was just beginning when I finally got there, and like some species of diurnal ground squirrel, I descended into the tunnels of the transit authority, and, as if carried along by crowds of the Elysian dead, was swept back down into the Underworld whence I had come.

Above me, above these tunnels filled with rushing herds of commuters, lay the surface of the little tadpole-shaped peninsula onto which, in the early decades of the seventeenth century, a small band of religiously motivated pioneers chose to live and dwell and have their being.

But how did it all come to pass? Why a peninsula? And whence came the hills and the freshwater springs and the three rivers running down to a deep-water harbor, and why the islands of the harbor, and why the deep layers of gravel and the rock foundations of granite below and the great waters beyond? How did it all begin?

CHAPTER TWO

Crossing Avalon

The Peopling of the Boston Basin

EACH AUTUMN on the Common, and over in the Fenway and the Riverway, and all down through the Arnold Arboretum to Franklin Park, in the deep little hollows in Allandale Woods, and even in the tiny gardens and backyards of Jamaica Plain, migratory birds begin moving across the Shawmut Peninsula and its environs. By the end of September golden-crowned kinglets, white-throated sparrows, palm warblers, and rusty blackbirds, mixed in with huge flocks of grackles and redwings, dart among the shrubs and flow across the skies at dusk in great dark rivers. Then, in the first weeks of October, winter birds begin moving in, the pine siskins, evening grosbeaks, and tree sparrows. The juncos come down from the north around the second or third week of the month. They'll stay for the rest of the winter, feeding in the Common and along the Fenway. By November snow buntings and horned larks and Lapland longspurs roll in and flit among the grassy verges of Logan Airport, followed in midwinter by flights of snowy owls

The birds are only one sign that the great wheel of the seasons, which affects even the most urbanized areas, is turning slowly, in spite of the general indifference of the human community. Insects were at work all over the city in those fading days of summer, with the asters and the joe-pye weed blooming in all the forgotten little empty lots and parklands, and the blister beetles feeding on goldenrods and the caterpillars of the red-humped apple worm foraging on blackberries in the weedy patches in the community gardens. Everywhere on the untrafficked roads of the Arnold Arboretum, the little woolly bear caterpillars were hurrying across the sun-warmed hardtop, headed for some nook or cranny where they would spend the winter. The trees of the Fenway and Franklin Park were festooned with the webs of the fall webworms, and on warm evenings you could still hear the katydids sounding out from the oak trees. From every weed patch, park, and green anywhere in the oblivious, otherwise cosmopolitan city, the meadow crickets and field crickets and snowy tree crickets were singing madly in a collective chorus, as if to hold at bay their inevitable demise in the coming cold.

On a cool October weekend not long after my circumambulation of the Shawmut, I undertook another, wider-ranging expedition just to see if I could gain some perspective on the deep history of Boston. Inasmuch as this little journey involved a motoring trip around the outskirts of a city known for its erratic drivers, the outing proved to be an arduous, even dangerous undertaking.

I began in the north, at the Middlesex Fells, an extensive 2,000-acre reservation of diverse habitats, with a high, wooded outcropping that overlooks the city. Then, weaving through back streets and blue highways, I worked my way west through a tedious landscape cluttered with strip malls and tract housing to Route 2 in Arlington.

Here I entered an even more treacherous territory in the form of the infamous Route 128, a heavily traveled ring road that circles the city. This was a Sunday, a day I had calculated to be generally free of trucks and traffic, and save for a few insane motorists who passed me at exceedingly high rates of speed, I completed that first part of the journey without incident, for the most part.

Northwest of the city I had crossed a number of small streams and rivers, including the Mystic. And on Route 128, at Wellesley and Weston, and then again at several other locations, I crossed the meandering loops of the Charles, which from the highway is generally obscured unless you know where to look. The great circle carried me south, then southeast through Canton to the highest point in the immediate area, the Great Blue Hill.

On this route, I drove by no less than six or seven major parks and open spaces that ring the city, although they are generally unnoticed by the innumerable commuters, tourists, local delivery trucks, and interstate semis that hammer along this circuit each day. But I also followed an even more obscure territory. Route 128 tracks, more or less, the geological demarcation of two ancient geological entities, the Nashoba Terrane and the more easterly and far larger Avalon Terrane, upon which the modern city of Boston is built. Stretching in a wide swath on either side of the highway as you work your way south toward the Great Blue Hill are a variety of road cuts that expose the underpinnings of the region, the outcroppings of ancient granites and mylonite, rocks that are often found in geological fault zones such as the region around Route 128. You also pass exposed sections of an igneous rock known as gabbro, as well as the banks of former glacial lakes and areas where immense, gouging rivers once ran.

Surrounded by a surprising number of cars for a Sunday morning, I entered the mainstream of the highway and drove along with the current, alternately watching the landscape and the sometimes unpredictable behavior of my fellow motorists.

The seasonal run of the three rivers that flow by Boston, the little departures and arrivals of the migratory birds, the flowerings and fadings and cricket calls, have occurred in and around the region for more than 8,000 years. Before that the land was cooler, there were fewer trees, and the world where Boston now sits was characterized by hardy little plants such as crowberry and juniper, and the fauna consisted of great lumbering things such as mastodons and woolly mammoths. Before that, say 25,000 years ago, there was no life at all, nothing but ice—ice for 60,000 years. And before there was ice there was fire.

But long before any of that, where the busy streets of Boston now burn, there was only the silence of a central sea, a great body of water known as Iapetus.

Stuck as we are in the tedious, day-by-day, hour-by-hour run of linear time, it may be hard to imagine, but in reality, the solid earth is as ephemeral as a cloud. Mountains once rose from the seas in the place that is now Boston and then eroded to hills; the hills flowed into the seas and the seas became land, and someday the rock lands will melt away again like a mist, and the seas will rise and cover all.

The story of Boston begins—if indeed it can be said to begin at any particular time in the 600-million-year continuum of New

England geological history—with the creation of a base of Dedham granites, formed in the mysteries of the Precambrian Era, when the shapes of the continental landforms as we now know them were all but indistinguishable. New England, or most of it anyway, was originally part of one of these early continents. It was a section of a great island arc of volcanoes located far to the east in what is now the western coast of northern Africa and southern Europe. Over the ages, carrying their payload of various rock formations, these shifting, primordial continental plates collided and rolled under and over one another, creating in the process geologically similar areas known as terranes. One of these, the Avalon Terrane, is where Boston is now located.

In the ages and eras that followed the Precambrian, whole oceans advanced and receded, filled, and then emptied again; mountain ranges as high as the Swiss Alps rose up in what is now New England and wore away to low, rounded hills. Layers of Braintree slates and Roxbury conglomerate, or puddingstone, were laid down under Boston, along with sections of Cambridge argillite, a slatelike rock, in the north and a layer of granites to the south, some of the oldest rocks in the Boston region. Ancient aquatic life forms scuttled across the floors of silent seas in these early eras. Carnivorous trilobites ranged through swaying forests of aquatic vegetation. Clamlike beasts known as brachiopods, mollusks, tiny shelled things called hyolithids, and ancient species of sponges lay on the sea floor. And then later, about 300 million years ago, in the late Paleozoic Era, starfish and brittle stars and corals and amphibian-like creatures known as tetrapods emerged onto the stage, and eventually (we are moving in unimaginable time frames here, millions of years in a second) land-dwelling plants evolved, whole forests of giant horsetails, immense ferns and club mosses the size of trees, with fissured trunks three feet in diameter, and also the earliest ancestors of conifers. And creeping through this vegetated track, the stuff of nightmares: hideous four-foot-long centipedes, millipedes, mites, and immense, long-legged spiders, as well as an abundance of mayflies and also cockroaches—a billion cockroaches—and giant dragonflies with five-foot wingspans, and warm fetid swamps everywhere on the low ground. Animals with backbones evolved, and fish, then amphibians, amphibians the size of crocodiles, and finally reptiles. Then suddenly (suddenly being a matter of a million years or so)—extinction, a vast dying off of many of the early forms of life.

But life bounds back, new species evolve, only to be followed by more extinctions—four mass extinctions in the earth's history, with many minor ones in between. And as a result of all this living and dying, a carboniferous rock known as coal was created, some fields of which can still be found along the shores of Massachusetts Bay and in Rhode Island.

All the while in these ancient eras, the restless earth was churning and breaking, with colliding continents and upwellings of terranes, forming high, jagged peaks. And there was fire and ice. Deep beneath the sea, near what is now West Roxbury, the great furnace that seethes beneath the crust of our little planet was building to a boil under the pressures of the surrounding conglomerate rocks and surface material. Finally, the fire broke through the crust in a chain of erupting volcanoes. Vast clouds of steam and smoke, lava bombs, and molten rock exploded out of the inner earth and blasted into the sky. Great billowing storms streamed forth, smoke plumed outward, and lightning and thunder and rain swept over the region. Eventually, the emerging lava was cooled by the waters of the surrounding seas and solidified, forming a hardened volcanic rock known as tuff, as well as the Braintree slates and Roxbury conglomerate and one of the most characteristic rocks of the area, Quincy granite, which was used for so many of the buildings and monuments of the city founded by John Winthrop and company.

Over in Mattapan, on the southeast side of the city, not far from Atlantic Hill and Nantasket Beach, you can still find remnants of these cataclysmic events. The city of Boston has preserved a small, two-acre pocket of land known as Woodhaven Park in an area that is curiously rich in the rocks that have been so much a part of the city's geological history. Here, under a grove of oaks and hickories, you can find the basalt and Cambridge argillite, the old heart of the underbase of the city, as well as Roxbury puddingstone and breccia, a conglomerate-like rock of volcanic origin.

The ages rolled on; the weight of the accumulated detritus of the volcanoes, the volcanic tuff, the granites and slates and gravel, the trap rock and felsite, slowly built up under the higher ridges of harder rock to the north, west, and south of the current city. According to the most prevalent of many evolving theories, slowly, under the weight of all the rock, the great block of earth below the ridges broke along a line of immense cracks known as faults. The huge land mass to the east of the fault line began to sink, and the very earth became as fluid as the sea and shuddered with powerful earthquakes as the land slipped. East of Route 128, the land slowly collapsed, while the hills to the west rose, and in the process a broad lowland some fourteen miles across was created, the Boston Basin.

You can see the outline of the basin from the top of the Prudential Building as you look north, west, or south. You can see it from Great Blue Hill or the Middlesex Fells. You can also see it from Arlington Heights in the west, just where Route 2 breaks through the granite hills.

One of these ridges took the shape of a great sickle, the so-called Boston Border Fault, which begins in the north at the Middlesex Fells and runs west along Arlington Heights and Prospect Hill, through Weston and Wellesley, and then along the north side of the Blue Hills.

It was along this upland that I was driving on that October Sunday.

Northwest of the city, I had had an easy drive—few trucks, reasonable drivers, and time enough to glance periodically at the passing road cuts. Some of the rocks I was passing were the oldest in the region—a band of 370-million-year-old granite near Wakefield, for example. Then, just south of Route 2, I began to hit heavier traffic. The barrage was introduced by a madman in a Porsche who imagined himself in the Grand Prix and blasted out from the Route 2 on-ramp without a glance and cut me off. I swerved to let him in, then cut back into the slow lane just in time to avoid another racecar that had materialized out of nowhere. The two were soon over the horizon, steaming through a stretch of mylonite and gabbro not far from Weston.

The speed limit on Route 128 ranges from 55 miles per hour to 65, but most drivers feel that it is necessary to travel at 85. This particular highway is no place for drivers of ancient vehicles of questionable performance such as mine. That year I was driving a 1982 Volvo I had bought from a cousin, a car so old and out of date that it still exhibited my cousin's Iran-Contra–era bumper stickers. Drivers on Route 128 do not appreciate such hindrances, and even though I was by then passing the Weston exit, wherein lies rich evidence of Precambrian shearings and upwellings and time scales so vast as to be unimaginable, I was forced to keep one eye on the rear-view mirror and the other on the road ahead. Not the time to contemplate the wonders of local geology.

Eventually, the period of volcanism and earthquakes and flooding that were part of the creation of the Boston Basin came to an end. For millions of years, rain and wind weathered the ridges down, and the land was slowly carved into its present form, more or less. Where the open waters of the Atlantic now roll, the flat floor of the basin—the current ocean bottom—stretched east for one hundred miles as dry land. And in the millennia before the coming of the last glacier, winding through this plain on its way to the distant sea was a great river, the ancestral grandmother of the Merrimack. The river ran down from the north, roughly along the lines of the Mystic River, not far from the present Mystic Lakes. It flowed across the basin to Boston Neck and surged along what is now Washington Street. The Charles River, smaller and straighter in those times, ran into the Merrimack around Allston, and there was another slow-flowing river in the area where the Neponset now runs.

This, then, is where Boston stood 140 million years ago, a product of drifting continents, of earthquakes, volcanoes, and erosion. But the final stage setting of the region was yet to come.

The orbit of the earth, as we are taught in seventh-grade classes in physical science, takes the form of an ellipse. At one season of the year—winter—the earth is close to the sun, whereas in summer, ironically, it is farther away. It is hot in summer, as we were taught, because the earth is tilted on its axis, so it receives a direct blast from the sun, whereas in winter it is tilted away at an angle and receives only oblique, weakened light.

But all is cycles—cycles within cycles, as it turns out—and because of these varying patterns of the earth's orbit there are periods, every 100,000 years or so, when the earth's relationship with its parent sun causes the whole planet to cool considerably. This series of cycles during which the orbit of the earth fluctuates, known as the Milankovitch cycles, has a dramatic effect on the seasons, or so it is believed. For long stretches of time, the seasons are extreme, with cold winters and very hot summers. Under these conditions, even though the snows build up each winter, the summers are hot enough to melt them away. But periodically the whole system cools down, so that the winters are somewhat warmer and the summers are cool. Whenever this happens—more or less every 100,000 years according to the theory—the ice that accumulates in winter does not melt away entirely in summer. As a result, a little more snow builds up the following winter. Then more snow the next year. And after a few decades the snows fail to melt in summer, and soon the accumulated snows are so deep and press down so hard upon the solid earth beneath that they form a base of ice that begins to expand southward and northward from the poles. As these dreadful, deathly walls of ice move, they crush the earth in their path, pick up seemingly immovable heavy boulders, ride over mountaintops, scour out river valleys, and press on inexorably. The ice, cut in tongues at the fringes, pushes ever southward, carrying its enormous payload of scraped earth and gravel and boulders.

The snows continue. The ice builds higher and higher, and deeper and deeper until it is more than a mile thick in some places and seemingly timeless in its advance. For millennium upon millennium it presses southward. Nothing can survive in this terrible season of chill; all life in the north exterminated, save in a few oddly situated pockets of protected uplands known as refugia. Almost all of the Northern and Southern hemispheres are dead land, with only a narrow band of life crowded into the equatorial regions in the sanctuary of the tropics.

And then, as subtly as it began, the orbit of the earth alters once more, and the seasons begin to change. About 20,000 years ago, the summers became warmer and managed, slowly, to melt away sections of the glacier. Year after year, generation after generation, for thousands of years, the ice melted. In spite of the hope and promise of better things to come, even this must have been a cataclysmic period in comparison to the deep, overbearing silence of the frozen world: thunderous roars of calving walls of heavy ice, the deep growl of roaring cataracts pouring over ice cliffs, streams and whole rivers gurgling beneath the ice like chattering voices, the crack of breaking ice sheets, the glassy shattering of pinnacles and peaks, and all along the shores of the Atlantic, the incessant cannonades of heavy surf battering at the ice walls, with measureless, mountain-sized icebergs breaking seaward in a surging wave to drift off and thaw in the warming seas to the south.

In the Northeast, where the glacier halted and drew back, it left behind its payload of sand and gravel, today's Long Island, Cape Cod, and the islands. As it retreated, it deposited immense blocks of ice that melted to form pools that are still with us today in the form of kettle-hole ponds. One of these, Jamaica Pond, served as the first reservoir in America.

Within the icy body of the glacier, serpentine rivers carrying loads of gravel, slowed and melted and left long winding ridges known as eskers, one of which snaked southward from the Mass Pike in Auburndale to the Riverside station of the Boston subway system. In some sections, deep holes developed in the ice, and within these holes the swirling waters carried sand and gravel and small boulders, which settled to form small pyramid-like hills known as kames, some of which can be found west of the city in Concord and Lincoln. And finally, as the body of the glacier retreated, it left behind a series of whale-backed hills known as drumlins, one of the most distinct land forms of the area. There are drumlins all through the city and out into the harbor and along the western side of the Boston Basin. Many were leveled for fill, but many remain, including the thirty-odd scattered islands in Boston Harbor.

One of the tallest of these drumlins, the future Beacon Hill, had a good base of water-saturated gravel and produced a series of upwelling springs. It was the presence of these springs that encouraged Blackstone to settle on the west side of Beacon Hill and later persuaded the Puritan flock of John Winthrop to move across the river from Charlestown, which had poor-quality, brackish water. Legend has it that good Mistress Winthrop herself, or more likely one of her servants, would go daily to a little spring on the eastern slopes of Beacon Hill, where Spring Lane is now located.

One of the worst sections of the Route 128 ring road, at least in my view, was, ironically, once one of the most scenic parts of this whole highway. Near Weston and Auburndale, the road crosses over the Charles River just where it makes a great oxbow loop and flows through a golf course. In earlier times—much earlier times—an immense glacial lake in this area extended south to Canton and the region around the Neponset River.

By the mid-nineteenth century the countryside here consisted of a scenic stretch of farms and pastures, with the quiet waters of the Charles River winding through. Now this is the point at which the Massachusetts Turnpike and Route 30 wheel over and under Route 128. The area is a great assembly of swirling, noisy, polluting traffic—hardly fit for boating or the contemplation of a rural landscape, were there any left to contemplate. In the early twentieth century, this was the location of the old Norumbega Park, which was constructed in the late 1890s and was a popular boating area for local Bostonians. At one point in the early 1900s, thousands of canoes, rowboats, and pedal boats would ply the river here on Sunday afternoons, their passengers drifting along, dressed in their summer whites, enjoying the cooling river breezes and the rural countryside. The old boathouse is still with us, and sometimes on hot summer days you can look down from the screaming highway and see a canoe floating on the blue waters beneath the Piranesi-like stack of highway ramps.

I would have liked to have the opportunity to at least pull off at some scenic overlook and meditate on the time scales that encompassed events such as the comings and goings of the great glaciers of the past, but no such spots exist on Route 128. In fact, there is no longer much to look at unless you are interested in the boxy, tedious architecture of electronics companies and technology research centers. In any case, given the number of on-ramps and the desperation of the speeding drivers then surrounding me, I was forced to concentrate on saving my own life.

At this point in my journey, I found myself pinned behind a shambling truck spewing noxious Carboniferous Period fumes into the otherwise fresh autumn air. The vehicle was moving at a slower pace than even I prefer, and the angry conductors of the cars behind me and on my left were working themselves up into a frenzy. I too would have liked to pass the beast, but every time I spotted a chance to pull out, another hornet would come darting up from behind to prevent passage. My car, as you might imagine, was not gifted with the most responsive pickup; it took a long time to get up to speed. Nevertheless, we rolled on, the smoking truck and I, and then, fortuitously perhaps, he pulled off. Then, near Dedham, I came upon a traditional 128 traffic jam.

Ironically, on these high-speed roads, I sometimes find relief in a little backup. You can drift along, stopping and starting, with no fear of tailgaters or high-velocity vehicles entering the highway. Poking along, stopping and starting, I had time to think about my geological mission on this journey.

Even before the glacier withdrew, there were a few hardy plants growing on the ice in summer months. The glacier had moved down in a series of advances, and in certain areas, after the younger ice melted back, the more ancient, insulated tongues of glacier remained in the landscape for as long as

3,000 years. But on the barren ground of bedrock and glacial drift and gravel beds, wind-borne seeds of trees and grasses blew in from the warm south, and a few plants managed to take hold. Then, in the short growing seasons of the postglacial summers, a few more seedlings were able to survive in the accumulated leaf litter and decaying remains of trees that had not survived the still intense, long winters. Some trees, such as white pine and eastern hemlock, may even have survived the glacier itself in the warmer refugia along sheltered coves and valleys of the eastern coastal plain. Hardy willows, birch, and aspen, white and black spruce, slowly moved northward at differing rates from the glacier-free region around the mouth of the Mississippi. These were followed by chestnuts, maples, hickories, and ash. Associated shrubs, such as shrub willows, ericaceous or heatherlike plants, and even southern species such as magnolias slowly gained a foothold. These species did not appear all at once; they spread by slow northward thrusts, died back, moved northward again, until finally they established themselves in the region around Boston.

About 8,000 years ago, Boston and its environs were covered with a rich forest of white pine, birch, spruce, hemlock, maples, beech, oak, hickory, and ash, underlain by a shrub layer of blueberry, huckleberry, buttonbush, ilex, and hazelnut, plus a dense, fertile mix of ground covers such a pipsissewa, club mosses, ferns, Indian pipes, wintergreen, hepaticas, and partridgeberries. Walk around the city of Boston today and look down the old, shaded, wet alleys, poke through vacant lots and the ill-tended portions of parks and playgrounds, or walk out the Fenway to Franklin Park or the Arnold Arboretum, and in those little sections where the groundsmen and the landscapers and the assiduous community gardeners have not evicted otherwise unwanted plants, you can still find the good old New England natives, the oaks and hickories and maples and hemlocks and the ancient native mosses and algae, liverworts, lichens, and club mosses that characterized the area where Boston now stands.

No sooner had these diverse plant communities established themselves than herbivorous grazers began to move northward over the North American continent, following the fresh greening of the trees, grasses, and shrubs. Grazing herds of caribou filled the steppelike plains and low hills below the as yet unmelted cliffs of the ice. Herds of woolly mammoths fed in the grassy scrublands, and giant mastodons, ten feet at the shoulder, fed in the emerging parklike forests. Also in the woodlands was an immense species of moose—the stag-moose—which had a huge, spreading rack of antlers. Here too was a massive forest musk ox, a beast akin to the tundra musk ox of our time; there were two species of bison, one a woodland grazer, and tapirs and peccaries and ground sloths. Tracking the herds came the predators—American lions, saber-toothed cats, dire wolves, and a large, fast-moving meat-eating species known as the short-faced bear. Cleaning up after these megabeasts was a variety of scavenging birds, vultures and condors with twelve-foot wingspans and teratorns, which were huge, perhaps flightless, vulturelike birds with thick, curved beaks.

Boston at this time was far from the sea. The glacier had bound up in ice all the waters of the world, but as it melted back, the released waters flooded over the land. Lakes and rivers were created, and worldwide sea levels began to rise. Living in the lakes and ponds around postglacial Boston were five-foot-long beavers, as well as many of the species of fish that are still with us today, such as trout and salmon and shad. In fact it is theorized that the anadromous fish of the Charles, such as the shad and the alewife, were originally land-locked species, which made their way to the sea only after the waters of the melting glacier flooded in. Their annual springtime migration is a return to their original territorial waters, the theory holds.

The islands of the harbor at this time were either dry hills rising above a flat plain consisting of grassy steppes, muskeg, tundra, or, depending on the prevailing climatic conditions, open woodlands that reached far out to the coast. Over a three- or four-thousand-year period, grazing in these various habitats below Tremont, Fort Hill, Copp's Hill, and the islands were herds of Pleistocene mammals, caribou, bison, and woolly mammoths. Then, about 11,000 years ago, a new species appeared on the scene, this one omnivorous and unspecialized.

Even before the ice walls had retreated, hunting along the base of the glacier and in some cases camping up in the valleys of green surrounded by ice walls was a mammal that was apparently new to the North American continent. It was a bipedal primate whose origins were African but which, through its ingenuity, its omnivorous, varied diet, and its ability to survive even in the harsh glacial conditions, had managed to spread across the globe and settle on every continent save Antarctica and North America.

When exactly *Homo sapiens* first made its appearance in North America is still debated among academic archeologists, amateurs, and native peoples. There is some evidence, still controversial, that there may have been Indians living on the continent even 40,000 years ago, during one of the 2,000- or

3,000-year-long glacial intervals. According to more generally accepted archeological theories, however, the so-called Native Americans were themselves immigrants, having migrated across the land bridge known as Beringia, which stretched between Siberia and Alaska about 15,000 years ago. That region, arid and free of ice, consisted of steppe and tundra and was populated at the time with game. Evidence is still being gathered, but it appears that over a period of some 4,000 years, small bands of these hunters, probably familially related tribes, moved across the land bridge to the American continent in two separate waves. The earlier arrivals crossed over the Brooks Range and the Rockies, which were then buried beneath the ice, then flowed down the West Coast and into South America. A later group turned eastward at some point as they traveled through the exposed passes between the Rockies and the Canadian Shield and migrated south to the shores of the Gulf of Mexico, then moved northward along the river valleys, such as the Mississippi. Still others carried on to the Atlantic coast and began following the migrating herds northward toward the ice-free grounds south of the glacier.

None of this was easy going during this postglacial period. There were broad lakes everywhere, raging torrents, and wide, nearly impassable rivers. Moreover, the people were moving through new terrain, without the untold millennia of cultural history to guide them through the unfamiliar landscape. The newcomers were able to adapt quickly to strange environments and to different and often rapidly changing climatic conditions. They pressed on across the continent, generation after generation, following the herds and the newly ice-free expanses of tundra and young forests. And finally, about 11,500 years ago, they reached Boston.

In this period in New England, to the northwest of Boston, where Lake Champlain is now located, there was a wide, deep arm of the Atlantic Ocean called the Champlain Sea. The Connecticut River was a long, narrow lake stretching from southern Connecticut to Saint Johnsbury, Vermont. Other rivers, such as the Charles, were swollen year-round, running hard, and thick with eroding silt sand and gravels. Lake edges were surrounded with impenetrable swamps and boggy marshes. North of Boston was a broad, sandy flatland where the Gulf of Maine now sits. Nantucket Sound and Long Island Sound were dry plains that stretched as far as one hundred miles east of the present-day shoreline.

Technically, the early bands of people were known as Paleo-Indians, and they were remarkably uniform in their culture. From the West Coast south to Arizona and all the way east to New England, they made exactly the same style of spear point, known to archeologists as the Clovis point, a five-inch-long chipped stone spearhead, often of flint, with a long groove running up either side from the base. Whether this groove was decorative or pragmatic is still debated. One theory holds that the groove encouraged the flow of blood from a speared animal.

The American Paleo-Indians were a primitive, undeveloped culture compared to their Cro-Magnon relatives back in Europe. Eleven thousand years ago in Europe, the Upper Paleolithic peoples of France, Spain, and Portugal were on the verge of developing agriculture and domesticating wild animals. Twenty-five thousand years earlier, they were accomplished enough in arts and crafts to have developed incised bone calendars to predict solar and lunar motions, and, as we know from the caves of Périgord, they were skilled painters of horses, bison, woolly mammoths, rhinos, and cave bears. They had an elaborate fertility-based matriarchal religion and produced finely carved female figurines, as well as decorative etchings on bones and antlers.

By contrast, the Siberian Americans (as they probably should be termed) exhibited few of these developments, or at least left behind little evidence of their handiwork. On the other hand, they were pioneers in the true sense of the word, the real discoverers of America, and unlike their more settled European brethren, they were up against a tough, unexplored environment.

The earliest evidence of Paleo-Indians around Boston is north of the city in the town of Ipswich, at a place called Bull Brook. In 1951 amateur archeologists, working in conjunction with Harvard archeologists, uncovered a large collection of Paleo artifacts, including many Clovis spear points. They excavated the area for the next eight years and in the end recovered what is one of the better-known Paleo sites in the country, which is ironic, since New England, because of its generally acidic soils, is not the best region for preservation of organic materials such as bone and wood. It's not clear whether the presence of these artifacts indicates that Bull Brook was a semi-permanent gathering site for Paleo peoples or whether it was a popular camping spot over the years. The fact remains that a lot of tools were left behind.

According to generally accepted theories, the Paleo-Indians, like many hunter-gatherer cultures before and since, followed the herds of game. After killing a large animal such as a woolly mammoth, they would camp at the spot and gorge themselves, eating and sleeping, until it was time for another hunt. They seemed to have a preference for hills. Hunters would collect on an eminence, review the landscape below, spot a herd of caribou or bison or mammoths, and set off on a chase. Newer, still untested hypotheses suggest that the bands may have remained in one area over a period of time and used much more plant material than was supposed earlier.

No Paleo artifacts have been found on the Shawmut Peninsula, but that does not mean that the Siberian Americans were not there from time to time. The peninsula was a series of high hills above a plain in their time and would have made a good lookout point, especially Beacon Hill. One can imagine a group of scouts gathered there, reviewing the landscape below for the dark rivers of moving caribou herds or the shadowy islands of grazing mammoths.

These people would have carried spears and a device known as an atalatal, a notched stick with a counterbalancing rock that served as a spear thrower. They would have dressed in skins and furs and straw-lined skin boots. Back in Europe, skins had been sewn for at least 15,000 years, and it is likely that our Siberian Americans wore suits of caribou or bison skin trimmed with fur. They camped in pit houses or tentlike shelters not unlike the Plains Indians' teepees—wood frames covered with skins. And if they were anything like their relatives back in Siberia, they may have formed the framework for their tents from woolly mammoth rib bones and tusks, of which there were probably many lying around on the steppes below Beacon Hill.

Elsewhere in North America, these Siberian immigrants would drive game over cliffs and then descend to feed as long as the meat was fresh. They would also use fires to herd animals into valleys and then slaughter them. But around Boston, there is no extant evidence of the practice. The Beacon Hill hunters probably tracked a selected prey animal, surrounded it, and brought it down with their Clovis-tipped spears.

The Paleo-Indian culture endured in the New England region for over 4,000 years. Then slowly—or perhaps abruptly because of an invasion by tribes to the west—the culture changed. The new cultural group, known to archeologists—although not to themselves—as the Archaic Indians, began about 8,000 years ago. Spear points became more diverse at this time, their camps were seemingly more permanent, and it appears that they had a concept of an afterlife. For the first time, archeologists find evidence of burial sites. The Archaic tribes began making more use of local plants, and the game they hunted was smaller—deer, turkeys, rabbits, elk, moose, and woodland bison and bear. They also began to fish. The forest composition then was, with a few exceptions, the same as the forest we see now around New England. At their campsites, archeologists find evidence of the use of nuts, such as hazelnuts, acorns, and hickory nuts, and also the seeds of herbaceous plants, such as goosefoot, which commonly grows in Boston's empty lots, along sidewalks, and beside the Charles River.

There was good reason for the changes in hunting tools and the use of plants. In the relatively short 4,000-year period between the arrival of the Siberian hunters and the appearance of the Archaic people, the large animals that the Paleo people had hunted, the so-called Pleistocene megafauna, abruptly disappeared. Gone were the great lumbering herds of woolly mammoths, the mastodons, the stag-moose, and their predators, the dire wolves and saber-toothed cats and the American lion and short-faced bear. In fact, except for wolves and mountain lions, there was only one large predator left, and that was the new bipedal primate from Siberia.

There is currently a debate in archeological circles over the disappearance of the Pleistocene megafauna. The standard thinking was that the animals became extinct because the climate and the habitat changed. But about thirty years ago a new theory was floated, suggesting that the Paleo-Indians themselves drove the Pleistocene fauna to extinction. The grazing animals of the American continent had never seen such a thing as a human being and therefore had no fear, and it was probably not difficult to select and isolate an individual and then kill it. This lack of fear, coupled with the Indians' intense hunting drives and excessive slaughters, caused the extinction of the large grazers. According to the theory, with their prey diminished, the predators also soon succumbed. This was a pattern that seems to have occurred earlier in Australia. The new immigrant Paleo people arrived on the continent, and the larger herbivores and predators became extinct.

There is good evidence for both theories. The climate did change, and woodlands began to take over other habitats such as the grassy steppes and tundra. But there is also good evidence of massive overkills, especially in the West: accumulations of mammoth bones and spear points at the base of cliffs, for example. Even into historic times, the Plains Indians maintained "buffalo jumps," cliffs and inclines over which they would drive the herds of buffalo.

For the next 5,000 years, with slight changes over time, the Archaic culture endured. Then, about 3,000 years ago, the Archaic people were either taken over or evolved into yet another culture, the so-called Woodland Indians. Like their predecessors, these people hunted deer and bear and beaver, but they were more skilled at arts and crafts and developed even more refined arrowheads. The spear as a hunting tool was replaced by the bow and arrow, with associated changes in the weight and structure of the arrow point. Pottery was introduced for the first time. The people began making bone- and stone-sculpted artifacts and, in the Northeast, began to construct more elaborate shelters, the most typical of which was the wigwam. But the greatest innovation of the Woodland people was agriculture.

Even though they were primarily hunters, the newly arrived Siberians must have consumed all the traditional foods of the Paleolithic diet: roots, tubers, berries, nuts, and leaves. The Archaic people expanded the variety of plants—or at least left behind more evidence in their camps. But the more sedentary Woodland people took plant gathering a step further and began to purposely alter the environment to promote the growth of certain food plants—burning the forest understory, for example, to increase the growth of blueberries. Then, about 3,000 years ago, along with trade items from the West, such as carved amulets in the shape of birds, came the seeds of an important native plant that had originally been cultivated in Mexico: corn. Soon the Woodland people added more crops from the West, such as beans and squash, and as a result, by about 1,000 years ago, they had adopted a new economy. They were still hunting and fishing and gathering wild plants, but they had developed a system of traditional agriculture to supplement their diet. They grew corn, beans, and squash—the so-called three sisters of Indian agriculture—to such an extent that the crops were not so much a supplement as a staple.

By the 1600s around Boston, these Eastern Woodland people had a common language and had organized themselves into the social groupings that we know of as tribes, which were loosely collected into larger, linguistically associated social groups known as confederations. One of these powerful coalitions, the Massachusett or, loosely translated, "people of the big hills," consisted of perhaps as many as 12,000 people. Like most of the other coastal tribes, the Massachusett were skilled farmers and fishermen. They had fields of corn and beans out on the Harbor Islands and extensive cleared fields in upland areas on the mainland, running down to the shores of the rivers and along the bay. During the colder seasons they moved inland and established hunting camps, made up of family groups living in separate wigwams. In some sections, they selected overhanging rock shelters and lived together in small groups. In spring they collected at certain sites along the Charles and Neponset rivers as soon as the anadromous fish began to run. By late spring they moved back to the coast to plant their cornfields, set up their fish weirs, hunt ducks and geese, and spend their days out on the flats gathering shellfish.

It was a simple, albeit enduring economic system, untroubled for the most part by the periodic plagues, famines, and devastating wars that swept over the European continent. The only troublesome diseases that the Indians seem to have suffered from was a form of tuberculosis that affected the bones, and the only wars they endured were temporary tribal conflicts and raids; there were no huge massacres of people of different religions, for example, and no squalid, suffering underclasses rising up to slaughter their oppressors. But after nearly 15,000 years, this way of life was about to come to an end.

These Eastern Woodland people were the Indians we all

know from European recorded histories. It was a tribe of Woodland people, the Pokanokets, who first met the Pilgrims at Plymouth. This was the culture that included for the first time clearly identified historical Native American figures, people such as Massasoit, Metacomet, Squanto, and Wetamoo.

As far as we can determine from the somewhat suspect English sources of the period, the people collected together in tribes with allegiances to a "king" (as the English phrased it) known as either a sachem or a sagamore in their language. The construct of the tribe may not have been as fixed as the English believed. Contemporary research suggests that people may have switched tribes often; in fact there may not have been tribes so much as linguistically associated people who allied themselves with a powerful leader, depending on which way the winds of war were blowing.

The tribe, or association, was ruled by consensus, which involved a lot of speechmaking, dancing, sharing of tobacco, and argument. And it appears that there may have been queens, or saunks, as well as kings. In the case of the territory around the Shawmut, the land was controlled by a saunk whose name was unrecorded by the English; she was known simply as Squaw Sachem, or "woman leader."

Leadership was apparently hereditary. For example, Metacomet, who changed his name to King Philip, was the son of the great Narrangansett sachem Massasoit, who dealt so kindly with the early Pilgrims before the relationship between the colonists and the Indians broke down and war started. Squaw Sachem was the wife of the powerful Massachusett sachem Nanapashemet, who, in the early seventeenth century, may have had dominion over a huge territory running from Weymouth in the south all the way northeast to Portsmouth, New Hampshire, and west to the Connecticut River. Nanapashemet was killed by the warlike Abenakis from the north in 1619, and since his two boys were very young at the time, his wife took over. It was Squaw Sachem who signed the deed to the land over to the Puritans.

The exact nature of this transaction is not entirely clear and may in fact not have been fully comprehended by either side back in the 1630s. The Indians had no traditional concept of the outright ownership of land. They practiced a system of usufruct, which is to say, temporary control or use of land rather than outright ownership, and it appears that the nature of the control was fluid, depending partly on the ecological conditions. At a yearly council, the leader of the tribe assigned the right to use portions of a territory to certain family groups, sometimes for overlapping purposes so that one family could hunt deer on a given tract but not pick the blueberries, whereas another family using the same tract could pick the blueberries but not hunt the deer. It seems that all controls were lifted, along the coast at least, when the anadromous fish runs were on. At these times Indians of various tribes, even those at war, would gather at falls and narrows to collect fish. When the runs were over, they would go back to their territories or back to war, whatever the case may have been.

Even the English were not as fixed on land ownership as we are in our time. The concept of actual title to land, that is, ownership in the sense of owning a book or a weapon, did not become fully operative in English common law until the middle of the seventeenth century. The Puritans would allow Indians to hunt on land that the Puritans "owned," even after a sale was determined. But once the land was under cultivation, the Indians had to stay away. Partly because of this vague definition, in some cases Indians sold the same plot of land to different parties two or even three times.

By the time of the Shawmut transaction, the whole Massachusett tribe, as well as many other local coastal tribes, had been decimated. Because of the internecine wars between the Indian groups, the introduction of European diseases, and to some extent the presence of the English, the whole structure of the Eastern Woodland culture was breaking down. Squaw Sachem's territory was sadly reduced; she was pressed by the Abenakis to the north and the powerful Narranganset to the south, not to mention that ancient threat to all the coastal tribes, the Iroquois confederation to the west. Squaw Sachem allied herself with the English, as had other Indian leaders before her. She traded with the renegade Thomas Morton at Merrymount and bought arms and tried to regain the loyalty of some of the villages that had given up their allegiance to her. By 1633, plague in the form of smallpox was again sweeping through the tribes. Down along the Neponset, the great chief Chickataubut died of the disease; two of Squaw Sachem's sons died. Down to as few as thirty or forty warriors, she finally sold most of her territory around what is today Boston to the English, saving a parcel just to the northwest around the Mystic River for herself and her paltry band of loyalists. By 1667 she and many other local leaders had signed a treaty of submission to King James, putting most of the territory around Massachusetts Bay under the jurisdiction of the Puritans.

Looking back over the disease-ridden villages and the ruins

of the former kingdom of the Indians, John Winthrop saw the hand of God at work: "the Lord hath cleared our title to what we posses," he wrote.

Southeast of Dedham, the traffic jam on Route 128 broke up and the drivers around me resumed their frenzied race. I stuck to the slow lane, as I always do, but massive SUVs and other vehicles created for high speed kept pressing from behind, driving no more than a few feet beyond my back bumper, cutting out at a sharp, swinging angle, and then slicing back in front of me, so close-hauled that I was forced to brake—which only served to bring up more racers from behind. But I plugged on determinedly, passing exits for Needham and Dedham and Westwood, and soon I could see the signature landmark of the whole Boston region in the distance, the eminence of the Great Blue Hill, the place that gave the name "Massachusetts" to the world.

This whole area was rich in early colonial history. The region was under the control of the powerful Massachusett sachem Chickataubut, who at one point battled the English because they had desecrated his mother's grave. Weymouth, to the east of the Blue Hills, was the site of Thomas Morton's Merrymount. Plymouth lay farther to the southeast, but the Pilgrims often journeyed north through the region. This section of the coast marked the boundary between the tribes to the south, the Massachusett people to the north, and the lesser groups that lived or traveled through the region each season.

For a while in the years after I came into Boston, I knew

a few descendants of the Eastern Woodland Indian people. I have since lost track of them; they were mostly peripatetic types, and they were elderly at the time, so I presume many of them are now dead. One was a hawk-faced man named Slow Turtle, aka John Peters; another, a weird, gambling, heavyset type with a pocked face, called himself Big Bear, and there was an energetic younger man at Plimoth Plantation who had taken the name Nanapashemet. Northwest of Boston, in Lowell, I met someone who called herself Turtle Woman, or Tonapasqua, and I used to know someone called Man Born Twice, and another named White Bird. To be only slightly cynical, I doubt that any of these people were related to the powerful Massachusett tribe that once held sway around Boston. Some of these Indians were from the extant Wampanoag tribe to the south, who managed to survive the various plagues and wars that affected their inland confreres. There was also a Nipmuck man in this group and an older, quieter gentleman who claimed to be related to the Pawtuckets, a group that had lived in or around one of the Christian Indian villages established in the 1650s by the so-called apostle to the Indians, John Eliot. And then there was my friend the entertaining Thomas Blackfish, who had wandered here from somewhere in the West and sometimes claimed descent from Nanapashemet himself, the slain husband of Squaw Sachem.

Long ago I learned to take all these Indian biographies with a grain of salt. Most of the members of the eastern tribes either died off in the seventeenth century or intermarried with local blacks and the so-called swamp Yankees, who lived in isolated rural communities around the Northeast. I realized that most of their stories were personalized myths that had helped these otherwise disenfranchised people find an identity for themselves. In any case, we all live by myths of one sort or another, and it is stories, after all, that create the reality of a person—or, for that matter, a place.

Very few of the Indian people I had met accepted the official archeological record of the emigration of the Siberian tribes across the Bering Strait land bridge. Thomas Blackfish used to tell me that, contrary to archeological evidence, his people have been in North America since the beginning of time, which, as I understand it, was (or is) a floating, indeterminate point, not necessarily measurable by the normal scale of hours, days, months, and years as we know them here in the West. In fact our whole science-based creation story, with its deep, 4- or 5-billion-year time line of the earth's long, lifeless gestation period, followed by ages of continental expansion and extinction, and the rising and falling of seas and glaciers, and even whole continents shifting over the round surface of the planet and periodically colliding with one another, does not fit with the story Mr. Blackfish's people tell.

In one version of the story, an island was suspended from the sky, and after many adventures and turns of fate, sky people took up residence there. In another version, the island was supported by a turtle. In another, the people were threatened by a huge serpent that lay beneath the waters of the earth. In many of the tales, there were floods that ran over the dry lands, much like the biblical story of Noah and his ark. In another story I heard often, at one time all the animals were huge and the people were small. They were threatened by the animals, but a mythic hero named Glooscap came down from the north and hid the people in a huge cedar tree. Then he went all around the earth and made the animals smaller, and then he took an ax and freed the people from the tree.

One hazy summer afternoon at the entrance to the Park Street subway station I heard yet another version of the creation of Boston, told to me with great enthusiasm by a gentleman named Walter. His story was even simpler.

The day I met him, Walter was dressed in dark trousers and a short-sleeved white-collared shirt, and he held in one hand a leather-bound book whose cover he repeatedly tapped and sometimes emphatically pounded as he spoke. He was preaching the word of God to the indifferent company of tourists, commuters, homeless people, and shoppers who wandered past. No one was listening except me. I felt sorry for poor Walter, alone in irreligious, rational Boston, declaiming his message to the empty air, so at a slight break in his monologue I asked him in all innocence if, given the time frames of creation that he had been outlining in his sermon, he could explain dinosaurs to me.

"By all means," he said solicitously. "Job. The Behemoth. 'He drinketh up rivers.' He's got the tail of a cedar tree—that's the cedar of Lebanon we're talking about, which was big. Very big. Sure sounds like a dinosaur to me. God made the world, see. Dinos and all."

I explained dully that my understanding, as I was taught in seventh grade, was that dinosaurs had died off 60 million years ago at a time when there were no human beings on earth, and yet he had just told me that his God had made the earth a mere six thousand years ago.

Walter lowered his Bible and shook his head and clucked sadly. "I know you learned that," he said. "I was told that too. But it just isn't right. There's some big errors in the scientific way of thinking. The scientists themselves will admit that to you. The fact is the earth is six thousand years old, and when God made the earth he put everything here in six days, and on the seventh day he rested. Now your dinosaurs. They were here too, just like Adam and Eve, only they died out in the Flood. That's what accounts for all those bones and fossils your scientists find. It's just that they're not that old. God made the dinosaur and there's records of them in the Bible."

Hereupon Walter opened his book, flipped through a few pages, and then ran his finger down the left margin of the left-hand page, stopped, and read aloud. "'feeds on the mountain, has bones of iron and stone.' If he wanted to he could drink up the Jordan River. That's the Behemoth, see, drinks up rivers."

He snapped the book shut. "There you go," he said. "Word of God."

Read as metaphor, there is perhaps some truth in all these creation myths; you could almost take your pick. Many of the stories that I heard from my Native American acquaintances were true in some ways. Their folklore followed, in a symbolic sort of way, the "official" geological and archeological histories of Boston. So does the Judeo-Christian model. The fact is there were great floods in prehistoric times, when the glaciers melted. There are sacred texts, folktales, and myths from around the world relating the event, most of them dating from the time of the great rising of the seas about 7,000 years ago. There were also Behemoths, huge monsters that drank with their long noses and sported tree-sized tusks. Five or six thousand years after their demise, mastodons or mammoths were still part of the mythologies of Western culture. And during the Pleistocene, human beings were indeed once decidedly smaller than most of the animals around them, as in Thomas Blackfish's tale of Glooscap's cedar tree.

As far as Boston is concerned, there are no specific creation myths. There is a Wampanoag story of a giant named Moshop or Marshop, who ate whales and plowed up the islands of Martha's Vineyard and Nantucket to the south, and maybe he came up to Boston and created a few islands in the harbor for practice. Oliver Wendell Holmes claims that the Roxbury puddingstone that is so common around the city resulted from a food fight. One day the naughty children of a giantess who lived over in Roxbury got to throwing huge blobs of plum pudding at one another, and the evidence is still lying around in Franklin Park. It's a good story, and more comprehensible than the geological facts, but it came along too late to make it into the probably more accurate preliterate folklore.

Night, mountaintops, and the tangled forest harbored any number of evil spirits and monsters in the hearts and minds of the Massachusett Indians. But at some point in the recent history of the Woodland people a new monster appeared on the horizon.

As with so many of the Indian myths and legends, the event is not fixed in linear time, but as we in the West measure time the event probably occurred at some point in the late 1500s. It may have been women who first witnessed it. They were perhaps working the cornfields on one of the outlying islands when they saw on the horizon a huge white bird or a strange fish approaching. They must have speculated as it grew closer: was it perhaps even their god Glooscap, or maybe Moshop, who rode on the back of a whale from time to time. The thing had high white squared-off wings, but as it grew closer they could see that it had the body of a dark whale or an immense canoe with high sides. Whatever it was, it came determinedly toward the shore, and when it was within the shelter of the nearby islands it halted and folded its wings and then miraculously (as some of the women must have thought at first) gave birth to a smaller whale, which also approached the shore. But this was no whale, as they could soon see; it was an odd canoe, paddled (backward no less!) by monsterlike people with beards and pale white faces.

The encounter is unrecorded, but what is known is that as early as the mid-1500s Basque and French fishermen were coasting along the North American shores, most of them fishing on the Grand Banks. Some of them must have explored the equally rich fishing grounds of Georges Bank and Stellwagen Bank to the southwest. From time to time, a few must have been caught in one of the vicious northeasterlies that sweep this coast, driven southwest before the storm, and fetched up in a good harbor fed by three rivers.

Whatever the case, at some point in the sixteenth century, European sailors came ashore and mixed with the Indians. Evidence of their presence turns up in archeological digs and stone carvings in southern New England and even—possibly—in an ancient stone tower in Newport, Rhode Island, that may have been associated with the early Portuguese explorer Gaspar Corte Real. Later, in 1620, when the Pilgrims first landed on Cape Cod, they dug up a few Indian graves, one of which contained the body of a blond-haired European sailor who had apparently gone native and had been living among the Indians.

These European voyagers left one other bit of evidence behind, unfortunately—a virus or bacteria to which the Indians had no resistance. In the years following the first contacts, plagues began to spread through the native villages of the East Coast. By 1620 the plague had decimated the populations of the northeastern tribes. The powerful Massachusett Indians may have been harder hit than some of the other groups. They were reduced by one third by the time John Winthrop arrived, and there were periodic epidemics after the English settled, as in the 1633 smallpox plague that killed Chickataubut.

In his free-ranging travels in the forests beyond the English settlements, Thomas Morton reports coming upon former villages in which no living inhabitants were left to bury the dead; bones and skulls lay scattered on the ground in what he described as a "new found Golgotha."

Then in 1675, as a result of land disputes, misunderstandings, and general distrust on both sides, King Philip's War broke out between the Indians and the colonists, who by this date actually outnumbered the local Indians. This conflict ultimately destroyed the local 11,000-year-old Eastern Woodland native culture that had evolved from the Siberians who followed the glaciers northward to the coast of Massachusetts Bay.

In Boston, the symbolic end came in August of 1675 on Deer Island in the harbor. John Eliot, a Christian missionary and defender of the Indians, had established sixteen Christian Indian villages around Boston by the time of King Philip's War. These converts were loyal to the English during the war, but in English eyes they were still Indians and living behind the lines, so to speak, and were untrustworthy. That August the General Court ordered that the Christian Indians be rounded up and transported to Deer Island—partly, it was argued, for their own protection from enemy Indians and vengeful English.

There was not much food, and it was cold; the women scavenged the flats for mussels and clams and whatever fare they could bring in, but over the course of the winter, in spite of John Eliot's pleas to have the internees fed and housed and clothed, many of them died of exposure or starvation.

The Indians were released toward the end of the war, but by then they were broken as a people and separated. They wandered inland to live out their time in the swamps or worked as servants in Boston—out of touch with their fellow tribal members.

God, Hobomacho, Moshop, or Chi' Manitou himself must have cursed Deer Island. After its use as what contemporary native people have come to call America's first concentration camp, the island was used to bury outcasts—Indians and, later, Irish paupers. At one point in its history, it housed orphans. It was used as a quarantine camp for arriving immigrants, it was military post for a while, and in the mid-twentieth century, it was used as a prison. Finally, and perhaps fittingly, given its history, in the 1990s it was chosen as the site for a new sewage treatment plant. This was in some ways the most positive use of the island since the time when it was farmed by the Indians, since the state-of-the-art plant at least helped clean up the formerly polluted waters of Boston Harbor.

There was a little flurry of opposition among the remnants of the Native American community around Boston when plans for the sewage treatment plant were announced. A loosely organized group of Indians that called itself the Muhucanuh Confederation banded together to protest the proposal and publicize the dark events that had taken place on the island in 1675. After nearly three years of struggle, during which construction of the plant proceeded, the confederation managed to persuade the city of Boston to admit to the atrocity and recognize the anniversary of Proclamation Day, the official edict in 1675 that required the Christian Indians to be rounded up. In August 1996 a celebration was organized by the mayor's office to remind Bostonians and others of past abuses of the natives. Having heard about the celebration from my native acquaintances, I went out to the island to join the event.

It was hot that day, and even though it was late summer, there were thick swarms of salt marsh mosquitoes and very little wind to drive them off. People had come from all over the country. Representatives from the local Wampanoag and Narragansett and Penobscot tribes were there, as well as a few from the dispersed group of Stockbridge Indians who had fled to the Midwest in the eighteenth century. There were no Massachusett people present, though, and no Pawtuckets—no members of tribes of the original people imprisoned there, in other words. Also in attendance, interestingly, were representatives from the German, English, and Canadian consulates. The English and North American contingents I could understand, but I was curious about the presence of the representative from Germany, so I asked him why he had come.

He glanced at me and then looked away at the horizon. "Germany is sensitive to this sort of thing," he said quietly.

There were many speeches by Boston officials and Indian tribal leaders that day. A gentleman from the mayor's office spoke movingly of what he called the genocide, even though he had been sent at the last minute to fill in for someone else and had probably never heard of the event until the week before. Unlike the mayor's representative, the assembled Indian speakers began each of their harangues with a long prayer to Mother Earth, delivered in their native tongues, and they burned kinnikinnick, their sacred herb, and spoke of the honor and greatness of their nations in their time and ended with more prayers to the sacred earth that supports us all, white and Indian alike.

If the Native American tenure in Boston could be said to have had a definitive end, or at least a definitively metaphorical end, it is likely that it took place on that day. Now all that remains on Deer Island in remembrance of the local Boston tribes is a paved trail running around the island and a plaque commemorating the event.

Just beyond the exit for Route 95 at Route 138 in Canton, I liberated myself without incident from the highway and drove north to Great Blue Hill. Here I parked my car, stretched my legs, and hiked up the red-dot trail directly to the summit to have a look back at the ancient geological basin I had just skirted.

As soon as you enter the woods on the southern slope, you begin crossing over sections of exposed bedrock. The granites here are smooth and rounded and look for all the world like the backs of immense rhinos or elephants. In other sections the rocks are broken into chunky blocks, and there are old roots and stunted white and red pines, as well as patches of blueberry and scattered groves of aspens and alders. This is a curiously rich geological and biological area for a site so close to the city. Among other things it is the highest spot within ten miles of the coast along the entire Atlantic seaboard. It is also home to an isolated and now threatened population of timber rattlesnakes, which den in the slopes of broken rock. But most important, Great Blue Hill is the site of an ancient volcano that burst forth about 440 million years ago and crystallized to form the famous greenish-tinted Quincy granite, which was such an important architectural element of the burgeoning city.

The ascent of this slope is easy, compared to many trails around New England—unless you are a small child. If you are, it may be a hard climb, but it is an entertaining, challenging one. There were many families out that autumn day, most of them descending the trail as I climbed, and the children were flushed and anxious to run, held back only by cautious parents.

At the summit is a blocky tower named for Charles Eliot, the founder of the now extinct Metropolitan District Commission, which originally managed many of the open spaces and parks around Boston. Looking north from the wide windows of the tower, I could see the landscape I had just driven along. Far to the north lay the high blot of the Middlesex Fells, with a line of high ground stretching east and west beyond. To the west lay Mount Wachusett, and inasmuch as this was a clear day with a northwest wind, I could see through my binoculars the singular peak of Monadnock. I could also see migrating hawks. Little dots—red-tailed hawks, ospreys, and what I think were sharp-shinned or Cooper's hawks—periodically materialized on the horizon and disappeared over the ridges.

Eastward was the blue harbor, with the green stretches of the islands and the peninsula of Nahant to the northeast. And there, lying in a flaming sea of autumnal colors ranging from green to yellows and brilliant reds, lay the city of Boston itself.

The city looked almost insignificant in that wide expanse, nearly overwhelmed by surrounding trees, its blocky towers crowded together as if seeking refuge from the sea and the wilderness surrounding it.

CHAPTER THREE

Forever England

A City Stripped of Hills

DECEMBER WAS UNUSUALLY warm that year. The quince trees put out new leaves, tricked into a false spring by the warming rays of the sun. Forsythias blossomed in the parks and back gardens, and in vacant lots over in East Boston and along the Charles the almond and cherry trees prepared to bloom. Lawn grasses on the Common and the fields and greenswards of the Arboretum stayed fresh, and the Fenway and Franklin Park took on a lush shade of green in the raking light. The white-throated sparrows stayed later than they usually do, and red-headed woodpeckers and Carolina wrens, normally more southerly species, were seen in Franklin Park by the Boston-based bird watchers. It was an odd year for birds: yellow warblers, myrtle warblers, and palm warblers, which generally feed on insects, were listed that year in the local Christmas bird counts. People were sunbathing on rooftops in the middle of the month, strollers along the Esplanade went coatless, and runners trotted along the riverbank stripped to shorts and T-shirts and ended their runs in a summer sweat.

I went down Commonwealth Avenue on one of those warm days with nothing more in mind than a good stroll and no particular destination except to see if I could find the old brownstone where my brother lived when I first came to Boston.

Passing along the streets of the Back Bay, which is the most orderly and regular street grid in this crooked city, I soon came to the corner of Fairfield Street, and there it stood, a Second Empire building with a mansard roof, inset with eyebrow windows. I could see his attic window, facing Fairfield, and it seemed to me that the building was in far better condition than it had been forty years ago.

Neither he nor I at that time were living particularly directed lives. My brother would occasionally manage to sell a large enough painting in one of the Newbury Street galleries to support himself for a while, and I was just back from Europe, where I had lived for a couple of years and attended school. At that point in my life I was merely drifting around visiting friends and allies in various cities and thinking to find a job at some point.

Even though he was a free agent, my brother would rise at a reasonable hour like any other working stiff and, in spite of the fact that he was repulsed by the claustrophobic T, take the line over to Chelsea Creek in East Boston to work on his boat. Once or twice I went with him to help out.

My brother had a girlfriend named Eve helping him with this project, a dark-haired woman with coal-black eyes who looked a little like a more delicate version of Sitting Bull. Together, like ants or frenetic beavers, the two of them scraped and sanded and caulked, replacing whole timbers and replanking sections of the hull, while the stolid older yard workers in their newsboy caps and stained coveralls stood watching, hands tucked in their upper pockets, occasionally proffering advice.

In point of fact, I think they were more interested in Eve than in the work.

Chelsea Creek was an oily little waterway back then, lined with rickety piers and filled with old wrecks and the ruins of formerly graceful yachts and sailing vessels as well as abandoned tugs and parts of sailing ships half submerged and preserved by the black oil. Esterhill's Boatyard, with its splintery, sagging docks, was no better, a graveyard for many classic vessels from the 1920s waiting to be stripped for parts before they were broken up. It was here among the doomed hulks that my brother, a habitué of aging boat yards, had found his dream.

It was a modest craft from the late 1930s with a double cabin fore and aft, lined with elegant windows, and with very little deck space. It had been out of the water for three winters and was judged to be too far gone and broken to be refloated. Everyone agreed that its time had come. But my brother could see, gleaming through the grime in the winter sunlight, her old mahogany rails and teak decks and was able to envision a perfect studio and houseboat. Never mind that she had no engine and her timbers were cracked.

The two old Esterhill brothers eventually took an interest in my brother's project and invited him into their informal work crew. They would all take lunch together—coffee boiled up on a Bunsen burner, with bread and sausages fried directly on the stove top without benefit of a frying pan. One day, in the back room where one of the Esterhills kept his bunk, my brother saw a huge rat. Mildly horrified, he informed the owners, who were at that moment indifferently slurping down their coffee and stuffing themselves with sausage sandwiches. They told him the rat was their pet and pointed to its food dish.

The types who came to visit the yard represented the underbelly of the old Boston waterfront, many of them survivors of the era when the city was still an active fishing port, and local husbands, brothers, and sons still died at sea in the winter storms of Georges Bank. The mast of a fishing schooner from this period lay beneath the pier at the yard, the vessel having been towed to port by the Esterhill brothers in the 1930s, after the crew froze to death in a winter storm.

Among this collection of characters, along with some honest fishermen and towboat operators, was an apparent madman with a penchant for guns, who was hauled away that winter in a police raid, as well as a few other drifters, watermen, and unemployed towboat operators. It says something about the nature of this crowd that one of the local captains once told my brother he preferred to hire murderers rather than thieves because the murderers were more loyal.

On days when I was visiting my brother in the Back Bay, I would wander over to the Common or go looking for coffee on Newbury Street, killing time until my friends woke up and the night festivities began. In time I began to expand these expeditions and wander down the Fenway or west along the Charles to a little woodland at the bend of the river near the Eliot Bridge. I remember on one of these outings coming upon an immense reptile out of the Jurassic Period. The thing had heaved itself up onto the banks of the Muddy River in the Fenway and halted, eyeing me suspiciously with golden eyes flecked with brown. Its plated shell was mossy and hung with algae and watery detritus, and I stood transfixed, never having seen any living thing of this sort in the wild. It was nothing more than a huge snapping turtle, but here, in the shadow of brownstones and banks and the refined Museum of Fine Arts, it seemed all the wilder, as if it had been caught in some bizarre time warp and accidentally emerged into the twentieth century from the fetid swamps and fern forests that once characterized this region.

I also remember a somewhat more aesthetic event near Jamaica Pond, not far from the Fenway and Back Bay. In a cove at the northern end of the pond, I saw a dark-bodied ducklike thing with a pure white hood, a bird so beautiful and exotic in appearance I thought it must have escaped from Franklin Park Zoo. It was a hooded merganser, a migratory duck that passes through Boston twice a year.

I knew nothing about nature in those days, but in many ways this was an advantage. All the world was a great beautiful mystery, and the wild things that appeared to me within the city of Boston were just that—wild, unearthly apparitions, somehow symbolic of a world beyond human comprehension. Thoreau, I learned later, felt the same way: "We need the tonic of wildness," he wrote.

I think what intrigued me the most was that this great primordial turtle and the beautiful hooded merganser and the swifts that flitted past my brother's attic window, chirping and twittering, on summer evenings seemed all the more wild for having made their way into heart of the city. I might not have paid much attention to them had I been out in the country.

On that warm December day, from Fairfield Street I followed a generally aimless course under the elms and oaks, then turned down to the river and walked along the green banks for a while. Then I turned back inland through the sadly diminished Charlesgate and the debouchment of the Muddy River, a practically unknown site in our time, having been obliterated, like so many natural features in this city, by highways. From here I crossed over the hard-running river channel of the Massachusetts Turnpike and ambled up the Fenway, listening to the birds and breathing in the odors of the wet autumn earth.

Halfway along, at a bridge crossing, an Asian couple approached me and asked in broken English if I knew the way to the Museum of Fine Arts. I told them how to get there and, having determined that they were from Japan, added that there was a good version of a Japanese garden outside the museum, created to honor the museum's former curator of Asian art.

They bowed and thanked me, and I bowed in return and practiced a little of my limited Japanese. This upset the formality of our interchange, and they bowed again, laughing this time, and said something in Japanese that I didn't catch. We laughed together and then I asked (in English) if they were enjoying their visit to Boston. They were indeed, they said. There were many parks, they said, which they especially liked. "Beautiful river," they said. "Many cherry trees."

"Also a monument to peace with Japan on the riverbank," I told them.

"All people," the man said, and then couldn't find the word for "one."

"All people," he said and brought his arms together and clasped his hands.

I was tempted to explain that during the Proclamation Day event I had attended on Deer Island most of the Native American speakers had made reference to the imprisonment of the Nisei, but I realized before I even began that this subject was perhaps too politically charged and too complicated to explain in any case. My new friend's English was not that well developed. Instead I tried to describe the Japanese garden at the museum, with its peaceful interior spaces and its diverse species of plants. I explained that the Japanese designer was particularly moved by the rough beauty of the New England coast, the rocky shores and the pines and sea vistas. In his design for the garden he had attempted to recreate this landscape in the small enclosed space.

"Many azaleas," I told my new acquaintances, "many Japanese maples and pines."

They bowed, and I bowed and pointed out the directions again, and we parted.

"Beautiful park here," the woman added as they left. She lifted both arms toward the trees.

As early as the end of the eighteenth century one of the first things visitors to Boston remarked upon was the general landscape in and around the city. Even in time of war, when he had other things on his mind (to say the least), George Washington found time to comment on the beauty of the place: the green hills, the small farms, and the town's clustered spires, beneath which his sworn enemy, the British regulars, were housed. It is interesting that, along with Rome and Paris, Boston is one of the few cities in modern history to have been occupied by enemy forces and not destroyed upon their departure.

By 1641 the Puritans, with little regard for aesthetics, had constructed windmills and roads, wharves and docks wherever they could, as well as millponds and ropewalks—long, narrow buildings where the lines for sailing ships were manufactured. For all their education (Puritan immigrants were generally better educated and more literate than their countrymen back in England), John Winthrop and his company were rough pioneers, fighting the harsh realities of survival in a generally unforgiving environment. It says something about the living conditions in pre-Contact New England that among some tribes January was known as the month of the Hunger Moon. Food supplies were at their lowest ebb, the weather was abominable, and it was a given that a certain number of elders would die in that hard season.

After 1640 the new colony was crowded along what is now Washington Street and State Street, near the freshwater spring in the area around Spring Lane. From the Long Wharf at the end of State Street, warehouses and shops and dwellings stretched south to Fort Hill and north to Copp's Hill.

The second little peninsula of the Shawmut, now known as the North End, was then almost an island itself, separated by the little tidal stream known as Mill Creek. The North End had become the thriving heart of the colonial city; shipyards and shops clustered on its shoreline, while the wealthier merchants lived side by side with the workers in a maze of alleys and lanes between the ferry landing to Charlestown and the area known as Dock Square. The South End, the southern part of the peninsula, was sparsely settled, with only a few scattered farms and cottages. Near the Common itself, still a bare, treeless grazing land, there were a few substantial estates, especially later in the century. But on the north side of the Tremount hills, a scraggly settlement called the West End sat cheek by jowl with a disreputable cluster of dwellings crowded together on what was known in the seventeenth century as Mount Whoredom, a warren of ill-constructed frame huts that served as the red-light district for the ever-so-pure Puritans. Even visiting foreign sailors and sea captains, a social group not known for prudishness, commented on the irony of the site in this Puritan city.

The better neighborhood lay on the northeastern flank of the hills, around Bowdoin Square. The ridges above the town were then uninhabited for the most part, but there were garden plots, orchards, and grazing lands over most of the peninsula, and nowhere in these cottages, farms, and estates were you very far from the sea. In fact the Neck itself, the slim connection to the body of the continent, was almost the sea, a forlorn place swept by winds and spray, flooded at spring tides, and lined on two sides by sucking mud flats. Rarely did anyone venture out that way after dark, and in the following century the Neck was fenced and gated. That which lay beyond seemed darker and more dangerous.

In spite of the colonists' development efforts and their intense religiosity, there were known signs of the Devil all about them in their city on a hill. It was Cotton Mather's opinion that New England was the Beast's own territory and that the Archdemon was infuriated when he perceived that people of God had settled here. Therefore he raised a company of fiends from the unseen world to employ their satanic devices to drive the people out. It was for this reason, Mather wrote, that the Devil sent out witches to torment the new settlements. Evidence of witchcraft was everywhere, even in Boston.

For example, at least three species of owls nested on the peninsula in the time of the Puritans: the barred owl, which favored swampy, treed hollows; the great-horned owl, which would have hunted through the last of the wooded areas; and the screech owl, which could have been found in any of the local habitats. Barn owls and long-eared owls and, in winter, even snowy owls from the Arctic, would have passed over the peninsula on their forays.

To the English Puritans this was dangerous stuff. Owls were considered ominous night creatures, associated with the Underworld and capable of predicting death. You couldn't even speak of owls in some sections of England without putting yourself at risk of a sorcerer's charm, and killing one was sure to bring on ill luck. Owls were known to be the colleagues of witches and associated with dark deeds. They were harbingers of death to come and were even used as ingredients in witches' brews. As most of the Puritans in Boston may have known (even though they eschewed theatrical performances), Shakespeare's weird sisters in *Macbeth* used an owlet's wing to strengthen their foul concoction, and in scene two of the second act an owl—"the fatal bellman"—shrieks as one of the many murders is carried out. Children in Puritan Boston must also have known the English legend that the owl was believed to be a pharaoh's daughter. In their time there was a little couplet to comfort children awakened at night by the owl's scream:

I was once a king's daughter, and sat on my father's knee,
But now I'm a poor hoolet, and hide in a hollow tree.

Along with the caterwauling, frightful whinnies, and hootings from the local owls, there were many terrible howlings and yowls echoing off the hills of the mainland each night, especially in autumn when the wolf families collected together. Like the owl, the wolf was considered a demonic beast and a known associate of witches and the Archdemon. Wolves populated the atavistic nightmares of adults and children alike.

The actual nature of this colonial wolf has been the subject of some discussion in recent years among wildlife biologists. There is a theory that the species of wolf that abounded in the region in the seventeenth century was actually a New England version of the southern red wolf, a smaller subspecies of the timber wolf that inhabits the West and Canada. In fact, some believe it is possible that the eastern coyote, which now ranges through the outlying boundaries of the city and makes periodic forays into the Fenway itself, is a descendant of the original New England wolf.

I spotted one of these "wolves" one night in a Brookline neighborhood: a quick flashing of eyes in headlights, a halt in mid-trot, pointy ears, triangular face. Were I of a different cast of mind, its appearance would have had all the appurtenances of the ancient wolf of nightmares.

I have also been awakened at two in the morning by the ghastly screaming caterwaul of a coyote, soon joined by others in its tribe. Listening to this fiendish chorus, abruptly awakened from the sleep of reason, I could easily understand why the sound would prove the existence of demons and devils.

The Puritans must also have heard, spilling off the hills of the mainland on certain nights during their mating season, the screeches and screams of wildcats and mountain lions, of which there were still a good number in the Shawmut area—yet more proof of the fiend-haunted wilderness that lay beyond. It certainly did not help that the Indians, another suspected ally of the devil, sometimes dressed in fur capes made of wildcat skins and, during battles with the English would let out gruesome cat screams. Nor could the fact that the heads of wolves were nailed to the fronts of churches in the region have helped dispel the myth of nature as the Devil—the enemy of God defeated and proudly displayed on the façade of his temple.

On at least one recorded occasion, one of the lowest and foulest of the savage band of fiends made its way into the very house of God on a Sunday. John Winthrop reports that in August of 1648, in the midst of a sermon by a certain pious elder named Mister Allen of Dedham, a snake crawled into the church and slithered among the seated elders in back of the pulpit. One of the church members pinned it with a staff and crushed its head. Since nothing occurred in the Puritan world that was not the work of the Lord, the event was considered highly symbolic. In subsequent analysis of the affair, it was determined that in his devious, serpentine form, the Devil had managed to insinuate himself into the house of God, only to have his head crushed by the righteous followers of Christ.

There were many such symbolic victories gleaned from the natural world. Some years earlier, in Watertown, witnesses had observed a battle between a snake and a mouse. After a seemingly eternal struggle, the mouse emerged victorious, a fact that was interpreted later in a sermon delivered in Boston: the snake was clearly the Devil; the victorious mouse was the company of faithful who had come seeking freedom in the new England. Satan would be overcome.

A mouse also served as the symbolic hero in another natural event when one of its tribe entered the library of a Puritan magistrate and, among the thousand books in his library, chose to shred the detested Anglican Book of Common Prayer, which was bound in a volume also containing the more acceptable Greek testament and the Book of Psalms. No other books were touched.

Such are the victories of the Lord, praise be His name. Such was the attitude of our Puritan fathers toward the natural world.

Their belief in what Cotton Mather called the unseen world extended even into the human community. Herbalists and midwives of their time, women who had brought over with them a working knowledge of beneficial wild plants, walked a fine line. They were considered useful in times of childbirth and illness, but that same knowledge, according to the Puritan mind, could be used for nefarious purposes—to summon the Devil, for example, or cast spells, or even poison people. In 1648, the same year that the serpent Devil made his appearance in the church, a woman named Margaret Jones was hanged on Boston Common as a witch. One of her sins was that her physics and medicines could have extraordinarily violent effects and would sometimes be turned against her patients rather than act as a cure, so the patient would never heal. According to the indictments against her, her victims' diseases "and hurts" continued unrelentingly and were incurable by all physicians and surgeons.

The fact is, the Puritans were up against what sometimes must have seemed insurmountable odds. Beyond Boston, the ancient wilderness of the English nightmare had yet to be tamed. Even as late as the 1650s, to venture across the river and through the hinterlands beyond the swampy shores of Fresh Pond, all atangle with silver maple and thickets of buttonbush, past Spy Pond, and on through the woods to the heights at Arlington, and thus westward to Concord, was to struggle through "dessarts" and swamps, tearing briarwoods and dark forests. There were paths through the forests in the interior in the time of the Puritans, mostly old Indian trails, probably used over centuries by the Massachusett people on their annual treks to and from the coasts. And there were tracks south to Wessagusett and Plymouth, and north to Salem and Newbury. But until 1639, when a continuous road was laid between Boston and Newbury, it was all narrow, overhung forest trails, unfit for wheeled vehicles and with no less than three unbridged rivers.

Even with the new road laid, it was hard going. Cotton Mather, with his seemingly anomalous interest in local natural history, journeyed up this road to Newbury in 1667 to see the two-headed amphibaena. It took Mather three days of hard travel to get there, and since (not surprisingly) he did not see the amphibaena, he had to turn around and trek back.

Also in this "waestland," as undeveloped wild land was known back in old England, quite apart from the bestiary of imagined creatures, there lived very real bears, wolves, wildcats, and mountain lions, as well as the animals they preyed upon, such as moose and deer and beaver. All these creatures were the familiars of the Indians and of the reprobate Anglican sinner and hunter Thomas Morton, who had the bad habit of periodically returning to Merrymount in the early years of English settlement even after his first banishment. But these wild creatures were still alien to the Puritans.

Trade with the Indians provided the Boston Puritans with furs and pelts and meat as well as baskets and seeds. But for the average village-dwelling Puritan on the peninsula, the world of Shawmut was becoming an orderly English village settlement. William Blackstone's apple trees must have borne well after the first decades, since by that time the Puritans had imported bees. Furthermore, from the Indians or the Pilgrims to the south or perhaps the likes of William Blackstone, the Puritans had learned the art of growing native crops such as corn, beans, and squash. They learned to fish, and they would hunt ducks and geese. Sailors in the community would make annual voyages to Sable Island off Nova Scotia to kill what they called "sea horses" for their oil and tusks. These were the last populations of the Atlantic walrus in the region. Over the next two centuries hunters drove them farther and farther north, and finally to the brink of extinction.

The sea mink, a larger, redder version of the freshwater mink, lived on the rocky shores of the outer islands of the harbor and was hunted to extinction for its furs, the fate of many of the marine species that had the misfortune to populate Massachusetts Bay. The Labrador duck, a beautiful black-and-white diving duck that frequented shallow bays and harbors, such as the estuary of the Charles, was a tempting target, even though their flesh was not all that tasty. Hunting pressure, which began in the early years of settlement, drove the birds to extinction by 1875. The great auk met a similar fate. These large, slow-moving, docile birds, a little like penguins, had been used as food by visiting mariners for decades, even before the arrival of the Puritans. As early as 1640, with the increasing European presence in New England waters, auks were in decline around Boston. By 1844 they were extinct.

Another staple came from the huge flocks of migratory shore birds that settled on the bays and flats of the Charles River and the marshes along the banks of the peninsula. Although ducks and geese were the first targets, Bostonians early on acquired a taste for the flesh of shorebirds, and over the next century hunting pressure, coupled with the filling of the marshes, which began as early as 1641, decimated the flocks. As a result, some of these species, such as the Eskimo curlew, are now rare or extinct.

Although not present in the vast numbers that would fly over the Midwest, passenger pigeons and more local birds, such as the now extinct heath hen, also made it onto the tables of Boston settlers. Heath hens were such common fare that at one point servants were driven to petition the authorities to limit the number of servings per week. Boston taverns and, later, restaurants and dining rooms continued to carry shore birds on their menus into our time. At the turn of the twentieth century, for example, Locke-Ober, one of the signature restaurants of the town, carried upland plovers and what they called doe birds (Eskimo curlews). It also served canvasback ducks, larded quail, and young black ducks. Markets were still offering shore birds into the twentieth century, and until international migratory bird protection laws prohibited the practice, songbirds were also consumed, although none were driven to extinction. In the early 1900s a single service from Taft's Hotel in nearby Winthrop gives a sense of the times. Listed on the menu, along with five species of local fish and clams, are local birds, including grouse and black duck, as well as teal, Eskimo curlew, plovers, woodcock, bobolinks, peeps (the name refers to some four different small shore birds, such as the semipalmated sandpiper), snipe, rails, and, as a specialty, hummingbirds served in nut shells. The "hummingbird" dish, it turns out, was false advertising; the birds were actually bank swallows.

Given this variety of available fare in seventeenth-century New England, the local Puritan diet was far better than that of their confreres back in England. In fact, troubled though they were with fluxes and agues, sprue, smallpox, and a host of similar, then-incurable ills, the northern colonists were actually in better health than their British compatriots, who at this time were suffocating in crowded cities and dying in the last wave of bubonic plague, which swept through London in 1666, killing nearly 100,000 people.

The Bostonians were also better off than the American colonists struggling to gain a footing in the South. Diseases such as malaria, blackwater fever, diphtheria, and the like knocked the southern colonies back repeatedly.

My expedition that day carried me farther out in the Back Bay Fens than I had intended to go. I had walked up the east side of the park, dawdling along to look at trees and stopping often to watch the geese and ducks in the Muddy River. A number of serious quarrels were going on that day in the duck world; on several occasions I noticed that two or three black ducks and mallards appeared to be squabbling and ganging up on a single duck, driving or chasing her (most likely) up and down the narrow banks, with a great deal of splashing and quacking. The fracas would periodically set the geese in flight, and they would rise and cruise off, honking indignantly, and settle farther downstream toward the Charles. Moving through the thickets on the banks on this unusually warm late afternoon were little flights of mostly unidentifiable sparrows, some of which, I noticed, were white-throats.

The sun was swinging low in its orbit in those last days of autumn, and the raking light stretched across the park, casting a network of skeletal shadows over the greensward. I walked back toward the river along the west side of the Fens, daydreaming and thinking vaguely to return to the nearest T stop. In time I came to the section of the park devoted to the Victory Gardens, and here I began weaving in a zigzag fashion along the little paths, now heading toward the Muddy River, now toward Kenmore Square, and all the while proceeding ever northward toward the Charles.

The Fenway Victory Gardens were laid out in 1942 in response to President Roosevelt's call to the public to plant more vegetables to supplement the nation's food supply. There were also victory gardens elsewhere in the city, including one on the Common and one in the Public Garden. After the war, partly through the efforts of Richard Parker, who led the fight to save the Fenway gardens from development (including one proposal to turn the area into a parking lot), the Victory Gardens were preserved and are still active today. Some of the plots are maintained by descendants of the original gardeners. In an interesting turn of events, Boston, which is famous for having garnered so many national "firsts," in the case of the Victory Gardens is famous for being last. It is now the only extant victory garden in the country.

There are seven acres of gardens with about forty-nine individual plots, all told, each reflecting to some degree the personality of the gardeners. Some are dense plantings of food crops, some are mini-landscapes devoted to flowering trees and shrubs and perennial and annual flowers, and others are a little of everything intertwined. Some gardeners set up tables and benches and chairs in their plots and spend the better part of a summer's day there.

Now, in December, most of the fruit trees were bare, a few

yellow leaves hanging on in the fading light. The sad remnants of summer abundance were still evident: old stalks of used-up broccoli, rat-nibbled cabbages, and brown twists of old tomato vines. The vegetable and flower plots had been put to bed, some more fastidiously than others, and although most of the summer furniture had been hauled away or stacked along garden fences, a few errant benches and overturned chairs remained, adding a poignant, declining air to the place.

In spite of the apparently lifeless state, however, the natural world in the garden was proceeding in its daily cycles. Little flights of sparrows came bursting through the brush and settled in a crab apple tree. A robin, clucking and flipping its wings, was preparing to roost in another fruit tree nearby, and overhead, flights of starlings came wheeling over in the gray, paling light to settle in the bare trees by the river. At one point, standing dumbly in the garden thinking about nothing, I heard an odd chattering, an almost musical sound, like the thousand voices of a distant crowd. South of me, above the trees, I saw a rolling block of dark birds rising and falling in a wave. As it approached, the flock rose and dipped and stretched out, and then bunched together again. It was a huge mixed flight of red-wings, rusty blackbirds, and grackles sweeping over the treetops of the Muddy River to settle in the thickets near the starlings.

I walked on, and in one of the plots I saw a dark mammal go scurrying past in the half-light, either a large rat or a muskrat. On other days here I had met gardeners who reported constant problems with raccoons and possums and woodchucks, as well as moles, rats, and mice. Along with these, although unseen by the gardeners, there were probably a few weasels and shrews and, although also unreported, there may have been a few milk snakes, which feed generally on mice, rats, and voles. It is also likely that the gardens have their share of garter snakes, brown snakes, hog-nosed snakes, and maybe even a few ribbon snakes, as well as red-bellied and ring-necked snakes—all of which occur in gardens at times and are listed as species commonly found within the city limits. In fact brown snakes seem to favor urban areas: they are reported more often in cities than in the suburbs or the countryside.

Urban gardens have been making a comeback; there are approximately 250 small community gardens and school gardens around the city, probably more private gardening efforts than there were during the Second World War, and maybe even since the early nineteenth century, when the Shawmut dwellers gave up on their own little garden plots and began to rely more and more on the produce from local farms just beyond the city.

In the 1950s, Boston, like other northeastern cities, began losing population, partly because of the combination of new highways leading out of the city and cheap federally guaranteed mortgages, which made it possible for city residents to purchase what they thought of as a place in the country. Eventually, there were so many of these rural retreats that they themselves became crowded together, forming the tedious and notorious American land-use pattern known as the suburb.

This flight from the city was not good for the urban environment. Houses were abandoned, crime and arson increased, vacant houses were demolished and not replaced, and there were many weed-choked, empty lots between decrepit dwellings, some of them formerly substantial single-family estates, now housing three or four large families. In the mid-1980s there were approximately 16,000 empty lots, a total of roughly 2,000 acres of open space. These were not pleasant yards, to say the least. Dead cars, litter, and drug paraphernalia, not to mention clandestine drug transactions and the occasional dead body, were the primary components, although I suppose on a broader scale a case could be made for wildlife. These uncultivated grounds of poor soil and rubble encouraged the growth of nonnative weeds and trees such as ailanthus and Norway maple and alien ragweed, tick trefoil, and garlic mustard. Wildlife is not concerned with aesthetics, however, and along with the rats that foraged in the garbage dumped in these spots, there were more acceptable species, such as garter snakes and brown snakes, possums, raccoons, white-footed mice, meadow voles, chipmunks, and, in a few lots at the edges of parks, even foxes. Sparrows, juncos, goldfinches, and other resident and migratory birds also settled here to feed on the seed heads.

One of the early experiments in the second flowering of Boston gardens started in Roxbury in the 1970s, under the direction of a man named Ed Cooper, who had grown up in the rural South and had come north in the 1930s, along with many other rural blacks, to find education and work. Cooper was a born organizer. Although he had vowed never to work again in a garden—he had grown up pulling weeds in his father's subsistence garden in North Carolina—he organized a group of elderly black locals to take over a vacant lot in Roxbury's Highland Park. At the time, the lot was strewn with litter and dead cars and overgrown with head-high weeds. It was also dangerous; some older residents had been mugged in the area. A few older men and women from the South, who like Cooper, had vowed never again to hoe turnips, joined the effort, and the idea took hold and spread. Cooper's community garden flourished.

With the success of that first garden, Cooper founded an organization called the Boston Urban Gardeners. The group began to expand, more local people joined, and in time the original garden, which came to be known simply as Cooper's Place, became a national model of urban transformation through community action. His organization grew over the years and continued to encourage the creation of garden plots in vacant lots in low-income areas.

A few years after this first success, another local organization, the Boston Natural Areas Network, was founded to help preserve the city's urban green spaces and coordinate the various gardening efforts. Then, in a curious turn in the usual scenario of paving paradise to put up a parking lot, another urban garden was carved out of an actual parking lot in the densely populated West Fenway neighborhood, not far from the Victory Gardens. The property had been used for parking cars since the 1920s, but through a neighborhood effort the land was donated to the city by the family that owned the property and turned into a small bird sanctuary called Rambler Park. The location was perfect for such a park. The Fens, just across the street, has over 200 different species of birds either nesting or passing through at various times throughout the year, and the trees, shrubs, vines, and flowers in the little park were chosen specifically to attract birds. White pines, sweet gums, and magnolias frame the space, and fruit-bearing shrubs such as crab apple, blueberry, hawthorn, dogwood, and cranberry viburnum fill the interstices, along with perennials such as bee balm and butterfly weed.

Darkness was falling across Boston as I made my way back down to the river, crossing through the high concrete walkways, bridges, traffic snarls, and noise that now characterize the area known as Charlesgate. I could see the wall of lights of the Prudential Building through the tree limbs to the east, and over the right riverbank, on my left, that modernist landmark of the city, the CITGO sign, cast an otherworldly glow above the town. Beyond, on the western horizon, a wide orange dusk was fading, and the sign stood before it, pulsing silently in garish red, blue, and white neon against the ribbons of soft gray, subdued reds, and orange light that was dying in the western sky.

The natives of this town have deified this brash commercial icon. In 1983, when CITGO moved to dismantle its neon advertisement, the people rose up in protest—an odd reaction, given that there had been a flurry of protest when the sign was first erected. The move says something about the nature of this particular city: its citizens are perhaps given to revolt, no matter what.

The city was founded in protest against the papist leanings of the Anglican church back in England. And once it was established, in spite of the generally indifferent attitude of the mother country, a group of rabble-rousers known as the Sons of Liberty rose up and began smashing all things British. Finally the colonists broke all ties to England and created a new nation—conceived in liberty and all that. And then, in what may have been its finest hour, Boston's citizens campaigned against the American institution of slavery, and the city became the center for the abolitionist movement. The market and meeting place known as Faneuil Hall, which had hosted the outcries of the original Sons of Liberty, invited equally inspiring orators such as Frederick Douglass to speak out.

Given these ideals, why would Boston residents—generally an environmentally sensitive group—seek to preserve the emblem of a petroleum company? As is well known, the overuse of fossil fuels has brought about some of the worst environmental practices in history, ranging from global problems, in the form of climate change, to local disasters, in the form of failed public transportation systems, air pollution, and oil spills, some of which were caused by Citgo itself.

In the end the protesters managed to persuade Citgo to save its sign.

In a way, I suppose, it was fitting to preserve the sign, but it was done for the wrong reasons. This angular, unnatural electronic blight raised above the otherwise low nineteenth-century skyline is a perfect symbol of all that went wrong in Boston in the 1950s, and in some ways all that has gone wrong in the environment since the invention of the internal combustion engine. Charlesgate, which I was then threading my way through, is a perfect example.

As the end of the nineteenth century approached, many public officials and private citizens began to lobby to have the Charles River and its banks transformed into a greenway that would contribute to the fitness and pleasure of the urban population, trapped as they were in increasingly unhealthy inner-city meanness. The result—with some adjustments—was the creation of a linear "water park," an open green space with promenades and greenswards that extended for nine miles along both banks. As part of the project, in order to halt the natural flow of the tides and keep the stinking tidal flats permanently drowned, in 1910 a dam was constructed near the mouth of the river at the base of Beacon Hill. By 1930, thanks to a generous donation from Helen Storrow, the widow of one of the major backers of the park project, James Jackson Storrow, the greenway was finally completed.

In her will, Helen Storrow specifically granted the funds to complete the riverside park on the condition that no road would ever be constructed through the greenway. But shortly after her death in 1949, the auto-maniacal city fathers saw fit to construct a public road anyway. Then, as if to add insult to injury, the city named it Storrow Drive.

At the confluence of the Muddy River with the Charles, the original park planner, Frederick Law Olmsted, had created a pleasant architectural water gate, complete with stone-arched bridges, channels, and landscaped plantings. But in the 1950s and '60s the entire concept of pedestrian flow between the city center and the riverbank—the original purpose of the green space—was destroyed by local highway construction, including, among other monstrosities, the Massachusetts Turnpike, which now runs cheek by jowl with Storrow Drive in some sections. The final blow came in 1966 with the construction of the Bowker Overpass down the middle of the former Charlesgate. This is now the least pleasant part of what remains of the riverside park.

It is only appropriate, I suppose, that this auto-ruined wasteland is crowned with a neon sign advertising fossil fuels.

Given the warmth of the evening and the lack of river winds, I decided to walk back to the Common along the water.

In many American cities an isolated park such as the Esplanade would perhaps not be the safest place for an after-dark stroll, but in fact Boston's green spaces experience fewer crimes than other parts of the city, according to police statistics. In any case, I was not entirely alone that evening. As I ambled along, I could see hunched figures making their way toward the river, carrying rolls of bedding. Some came plodding westward from the heart of the city, some appeared from the various pedestrian bridges over Storrow Drive, and some seemed to have materialized from the grassy banks of the river. These harmless, temporarily homeless individuals were headed for their night quarters under the highway overpasses and bridges.

I had noticed on earlier expeditions along the riverbank that some of these unfortunates stored their few worldly goods in small bundles in selected places under the bridges and returned to their spot each night. I had also seen other semipermanent camping places in semiwild, isolated areas all around the city. A few years ago, a homeless man constructed a veritable English wigwam in the woods at the bend of the Charles near the Eliot Bridge. It was a fine structure, with low walls of locally collected stones, a wood frame, and plastic sheeting as roofing. Unfortunately, he did not have an official building permit and was camped illegally on state property, and reluctantly the state, being the state, was forced to evict him. Officials hired prisoners to tear the building down, one of whom, I heard, said he fully expected to go to hell, not for his original crime, but because of the work he was doing.

One of these itinerant individuals passed close by me as I walked along, and it seemed appropriate, inasmuch as we were the only ones abroad in that place at that particular moment, to wish him good night. He stopped in midstride and looked over at me curiously.

"What did you say?" he asked incredulously.

"Just good night," I said. "Not a bad night tonight. Not too cold."

"Good night to you, then," he mumbled and shuffled on. I think he was totally mystified.

Two minutes later a low, scurrying shadow crossed my path. A little farther down the river I saw another. Then another. These were brown rats, *Rattus norvegicus,* the most common mammal in the city besides the equally ubiquitous *Homo sapiens.*

As far as I know, there has never been a census of the rat population of Boston, but in other American cities, such as New York, population surveys have claimed one rat per person, which according to rat experts turns out to be urban folklore. People still outnumber rats, even in New York. But Boston is a waterfront city with many old buildings, a perfect environment for rats, and as anyone who spends any time on the streets after hours will attest, rats are everywhere.

Urban legend also held that while the Central Artery Project was under construction, evicted rats were uprooted from their tunnels and warrens and overran the city, but in fact the project managers had instituted a rat extermination program even before construction began and had eliminated (probably) most of the rats.

There were no brown rats on the Shawmut Peninsula in the time of Squaw Sachem. Depending on the variable climate conditions, there may have been a few rats around in colonial days, but these would have been a native species known as the wood rat, a benign beast with a furry tail, unlike the brown rat, which has a naked tail. Wood rats are not generally associated with human habitation, although they do seem to have a predilection for shiny things, such as silver buttons and coins. Also known as pack rats, or trade rats, they will carry off rings and diamonds and earrings if they get a chance, to decorate their nests. But they're fair-minded creatures and will often leave something in its place—a pebble, for example. One could, I suppose, write a thesis on the primordial nature of aesthetics given this fact. There must be a universal lesson buried somewhere.

Black rats, which are also associated with human habitation, may have come to Boston with John Winthrop's fleet, since they seem to favor waterfronts and ships. They may even have arrived earlier with the fishermen or traders such as William Blackstone, but they were driven out by the more aggressive brown rats, which arrived in the city with British merchant ships in the eighteenth century. Black rats don't do well in cold, in any case, and are now more common in southern regions.

Brown rats probably evolved in Asia and spread all across Europe following the trade routes. They are notoriously fast and successful breeders and have a wide, omnivorous diet; garbage, which normally contains a variety of delicacies and choices, appears to be one of their favorite foods, although in nature they would probably prefer cereals. They're good swimmers, they make extensive burrows, and they're smart. They were successfully crossbred to create the white rat used in laboratories and are perhaps one of the more studied mammals in science.

All along my walk back to the Common, the rats appeared and disappeared. They were determined in their passage, intent on whatever mission they had set out on, and in no way like their fellow rodents, the halting, half-tame gray squirrels of the Common, who race forward, stop in mid-dash, and sit up, thinking what to do next.

It was by then pitch dark. The city lights were burning ahead of me in the calm air, the waters of the river were softly lapping at the shores, reflecting the lights in broken ripples, and lines of car lights were passing to and fro over the bridges. This was mid-December, darkness had come in early, and the infamous human rat race of commuters was in full bore. Storrow Drive, to my right, was crowded with west-bound automobiles—double-eyed snakes steadily crawling over the landscape.

Walking along, lost in thought, I remembered some years earlier riding home on Storrow Drive at this section of the river after returning on a late-night flight from Europe. I had been in many European river cities in the days before and had spent a number of evenings strolling along the banks of the Tiber and the Arno and the Thames. On the way home from the airport, totally fatigued (it was about three in the morning in my time frame), I fell asleep in the back seat of the car. I woke up again on the shores of a river and looked out at the landscape.

The horizon was dark, and the lights of the low buildings along the river were winking against the black waters and glowing through a soft fog. I squinted out the window at the details of the scene: tree-lined riverbank, London plane trees in silhouette. We passed a few stone-arched bridges. Dark water, the gleam of soft lights. A grassy verge on our side of the river. More lines of trees, their bare, wet branches passing the car window in a stately procession. I squinted again and tried to wake up. Where were we? What river was this? What city? What quiet, unassuming, low-key environment were we now sailing past? I had to review the recent flight of days to realize that we had crossed the Atlantic and were now in the American city known as Boston.

I have hosted various guests from Europe over the years, and to entertain them I have taken them to the usual tourist sites: the Common, the Freedom Trail, the back streets of Beacon Hill, and other historic attractions. Generally speaking, they have been singularly unimpressed. Similarly, over the years, I have fallen into conversation with European tourists in the city and have noticed that although they like very much the humane scale of the city—especially in comparison to New York or Miami—they do not seem particularly surprised by the place. I once was asked to guide a contingent of visiting Swedes through the town. Also unimpressed. On another occasion I took an international group of visiting diplomats around the city. Same reaction. The general consensus seemed to be that Boston was familiar territory for them, more like a continental city—most like London, in fact.

This is not necessarily surprising. Boston was, after all, a British town for nearly 150 years, and as the community expanded in the early years, its builders naturally looked to England for models. After the Great Fire of 1666, London itself was rebuilt under the direction of Christopher Wren, who introduced Baroque forms into English architecture, soon followed by a revival of Palladian traditions and the arrival of Neoclassical designs. New England, which tended to lag behind in these architectural developments, continued to follow the old Elizabethan designs well into the eighteenth century. In any case, save for a few buildings such as Faneuil Hall and King's Chapel, early Boston was not built by trained architects but by skilled craftsmen whose design ideas came from old pattern books that for the most part mimicked popular models back in England.

The peninsula itself was expanding in those hopeful early decades. By 1641 the legislature had granted title to the shoreline to a group of merchants to build wharves and docks and warehouses around the area where Faneuil Hall now stands. Then, in 1643, a group of developers was given permission to extend a spit of land across North Cove to form a millpond and then cut a waterway along what is now Blackstone Street, in order to create grist mills to grind grain. Over the next few decades, the mud flats along the shorelines were filled and developed, sea walls were constructed, builders threw a barricade up across South Cove for the defense of the town, forts and windmills were built, and the wetlands along the Neck were filled to widen the strip of land. Long Wharf was constructed in 1710, and then in 1740 the artist and architect John Smibert designed Faneuil Hall. Also during this same period, in 1723, Christ Church in the North End was constructed, now the oldest surviving church in the city.

Boston was spreading outward across the peninsula. By 1776 development covered a quarter of the 1,100 acres of the Shawmut. On prominent corners around Beacon Hill, elegant Georgian mansions of stone or painted clapboards or red brick surrounded leafy squares, and most of the larger houses had lush gardens of vegetables and flowers and even small orchards. As many as twelve steeples and spires pierced the skyline, and below the churches and public buildings, in the narrow lanes and open byways, there were no less than thirty establishments and public houses serving good New England rum, locally distilled from Cuban molasses.

Like London, Boston began in this period to construct garden squares as it developed. This urban land-use pattern consisted of small neighborhoods constructed around a public open space, generally landscaped with trees, flower beds, and greenswards, and tended by the city or by the local residents. Some of these squares in London, such as Eccleston Square, a renowned three-acre private park in the heart of the city, are now major garden spots run by the residents and overseen by an attendant gardener.

The first such square in Boston was Franklin Place, located around Arch Street and Franklin Street, in today's downtown section. Later Louisburg Square and Pemberton Square were developed, and later still, in the South End, a whole series of garden squares was created, including Blackstone Square, Worcester Square, and Chester Square. These were originally tranquil refuges set with leafy trees, sparkling fountains, and, as in Chester Square, a mall, with a double row of elms and finely crafted wrought-iron fences.

In the late eighteenth century, the innovative American architect and Boston selectman Charles Bulfinch was involved in a few of these designs. Bulfinch had traveled abroad and made notes on architectural developments in England and Europe, and he did his best to introduce the Neoclassical style to the city. Over time he managed to persuade the town officials to accept many, if not all, of the British innovations, and the resulting combination was what is now referred to as the Federal style, characterized by the low-pitched roofs, fanlights, and bowed bays that gave the early-nineteenth-century city its character.

As early as 1698 Boston had established itself as the largest town in British North America. Its port was the busiest in the colonies, outstripping those in both Scotland and Ireland. By the early nineteenth century, the harbor was a forest of masts, the wharves were scented with tar and oranges mingled with salt air and crowded with chandleries, ropewalks, canvas manufacturers, and shipyards, as well as taverns and grog shops, and, until 1807, when it was cleared, the questionable pleasures of Mount Whoredom.

The town itself was thick with artisans and tradesmen, as well as merchants, lawyers, bankers, physicians, and clergy. And yet Boston was still a contained community, not fully built out, with pastures and windy hills, orchards and peaceful cows grazing on the Common, and all the amenities of space, air, and light, which later in the century were to become such premiums. People going west from this bustling town would travel the cart track along the Neck out to Roxbury and on to Brookline or, alternatively, take the ferry over to Charlestown and follow the road out to Cambridge and beyond—the course taken by the British regulars on that fateful April night in 1775. Then in 1786 a bridge was built over the river to Cambridge, the cart track to Roxbury was improved, and slowly, decade by decade, development rolled westward.

Although they did not burn or bomb the city when they evacuated Boston in March of 1776, the British did manage to despoil the town. They tore out church pews for firewood, drank up the best wines from the estate wine cellars, broke windows, and, in vengeance, just before they left, cut down the ancient oaks around the Common. Following this, during the war years, there was a general economic decline in Boston. But by the end of the century, the city sprang back, and by the early 1800s it was among the richest trading ports in the world.

In the early years of the colony Boston was exporting fish, fur, and lumber, which legally could be traded only with England, although in fact the exporters did business wherever they could. But after the war, Boston trade routes reached to South America, Africa, and Europe; its outbound ships carried cod and corn, clapboards and rum, and brought home indigo, sugar, Madeira, oranges, lemons, and grapes. After the opening of the China trade, the port began to send its sleek-hulled clipper ships around the Horn and up the California coast to the Northwest for sea-otter pelts, then out to Hawaii for sandalwood, and thence to China, and then, two or three years later, back through the Narrows to home port, laden with tea and silks and fine porcelain. It was in these ambitious midcentury years that Charles McKay's East Boston shipyard turned out that glory of the seas, the *Flying Cloud*, which so inspired my little landlocked family in the 1950s. She was 229 feet on the deck, built of the finest oak and pine, with masts that towered 88 feet into the Boston skies, and she had a figurehead of a winged angel blowing a trumpet. And in fact there was much to trumpet. The city was experiencing some of its finest decades.

All these brave new developments may have been good for the economy, but they were not necessarily good for the environment. More and more of the ecologically critical marshlands along the riverbanks and the harbor and bay were filled for development, thus evicting forever the myriad snails, crabs, juvenile fish, sprat, and fry that were at the base of the food chain of the deep-water marine environment and the fishing industry upon which the city relied. The wetlands also buffered the battering storms that hammered the city between November and March, and upstream, in the watersheds of the Charles, the Neponset, and the Mystic, absorbed the excess waters that caused downstream flooding.

Pollution controls, needless to say, were nonexistent in those early years, and with the construction of new mills, butcheries, tanning operations, fish-processing plants, and distilleries, the waters of the Charles became sadly contaminated and continued to decline well into the twentieth century. The once pristine flats, which for thousands of years had provided shellfish for both the Indians and the English, became stinking morasses that offended the noses of downwind residents twice a day, at low tide. The little rivers and streams that fed the Charles and the harbor carried an appalling, odoriferous load of pollutants day after day, year after year. One such small stream, north of the city, carried a unique form of offal from a meat-processing plant—discarded pig heads. The stream was so repulsive and the local airs so foul that the city fathers could think of no other solution than to bury it altogether: the normal pattern in the city's development. If thine environment offend thee, strike it out.

The expansion continued, acre by acre, marsh by marsh, in an almost amoeba-like growth, until the original shape of the Shawmut Peninsula was so obliterated and so obscured by wharves and docks, streets, dwellings, markets, meetinghouses, and made lands that old William Blackstone, were he to come riding back on his brindle bull, would not know the place. Boston had joined that company of Western European cities that had struggled up from low, wet places, a Rome built at the edges of the Pontine marshes, an Amsterdam saved by sea walls, or a New World Venice set upon pilings.

In its early years, Boston society, as in the mother country, seems to have been somewhat splintered. Half of its members were rich, pleasure-seeking, high-living Anglicans, while the other half (also rich) were clean-living, church-going Puritans, with a few pragmatic, liberty-hungry merchants and lawyers in between. The conflicting doctrines had been there from the very beginning. William Blackstone himself was an Anglican minister, but he had withdrawn to the freedom of wilderness so that he might, as he said, "be as free from the governance of the Puritans, as that of the King."

By the turn of the nineteenth century the old Puritans, in spite of their overweening sumptuary laws, were losing ground to Anglicans and Baptists, Quakers and other sects, and, among the intellectuals, even a few churchless deists with hardly any organized religious associations.

It was out of this conflicting mélange that a certain principled and upright Bostonian character emerged and held the political reins of the city until the twentieth century: the one hundred or so families nicknamed the Boston Brahmins by Oliver Wendell Holmes. This was an educated body of the city's populace; they were mercantile and sharp, even avaricious. But they were also moral and square, unostentatious and principled. They had within them a deep vein of the old Puritan work ethic and were not given to retirement or sport or idle entertainments. They saved their money and lived in clapboard houses and did not build mansions in Newport to escape from their city; in fact they did not travel much. "Why travel," one of them said, "when we are already here?" They were highly literate, they appreciated education, and they were cultured. The merchants of the previous generation had made their money in occasionally questionable international trades such as slaves and opium and had constructed dark satanic mills beyond the city, but their children fell back on their old Puritan roots and put their money to moral purpose, setting up municipal lodging houses for the indigent, settlement houses, relief payments to the poor, a great American library, an innovative sewer system, and public baths. In fact, partly because they settled here so early in North American history, they built the first of almost everything: the first schools and universities and libraries, early printing presses, newspapers, and bookshops, the first symphony orchestra, a world-class art museum. They also fostered the first authentic American literary voice. At one point in the late nineteenth century, Boston was populated with so many authors that one visiting writer from the West claimed you could not fire a revolver in the city without bringing down the author of a three-volume work. The principled Brahmins and their fellow travelers were the prime movers of the abolition movement, among other causes. They encouraged huge antislavery demonstrations on the Common, raised the first all-black infantry regiment, with one of their own children at its head, and turned out 40,000 citizens on the streets to protest the return to the South of a single captured escaped slave.

And almost in spite of themselves, when they finally opened their eyes and realized what their mad dash of trade and industry and progress had wrought upon their beloved city on a hill, they became the first force of American conservation.

CHAPTER FOUR

Ring of Green

Restoring the Shawmut

JANUARY CAME DOWN upon us then with a glacial vengeance, as if to make up for simpering December. Snows fell. Snow upon snow. Then an icy rain, and after that a frost so deep the world turned to crystal. Wandering under the trees of the Public Garden or the Arboretum, you might easily believe that the whole bright city on a hill had finally come to fruition and had lost all contact with the base earth and ascended into heaven, just as John Winthrop would have wished. But then it rained again, and the world darkened into a November-like gloom for a few days, with a cold wind flecked with snow driving down from the northeast, stripping umbrellas and forcing the good workers of this city to crouch along the dripping walls, hands to collars against the blasts.

You could not get warm in those few days. The chill crept into the inner sanctums of museums and libraries, it burrowed into apartments and frame houses and lingered in little icy pools by windows and doors. Outside, flights of sparrows and starlings swept along the river like stray leaves. The juncos in the Fenway flashed white underwings in the periodic blasts and sailed off across the frozen grounds. Out at Logan Airport, snowy owls hunched in the brown, whipping grasses, feathers ruffled, waiting for prey, and little wind-blown flocks of larks and snow buntings rose and fell and rose again. And everywhere, wind. Wind moaning at the eaves. Wind channeling down the city's canyon walls. Wind barking and howling at night and sending spray up over the sea walls and wharves and docks. Only the sea birds were happy in those bitter days. Flocks of little buffleheads and scaup bounced on the whitecaps on the lower reaches of the Charles and on the still open waters of Jamaica Pond. The herring gulls and ring-billed gulls tipped between the high-rises of the financial district like escaped kites. Arctic visitors were spotted off Dorchester Bay: Iceland gulls, a glaucous gull, a kittiwake. Also gannets, red-throated loons, and, out in the harbor, flocks of eiders and brant in little flotillas like an invading armada, their straight black necks crowded together like masts. Farther offshore, beyond the Brewsters, stormy petrels, skuas, and jaegers, as well as the usual collections of murres, dovekies, razorbills, and guillemots skipped and dove among the gray waves.

And then the wind dropped and the customary thankless chill of the seemingly endless Boston winter set in.

On one of those bitterly cold, jet-black nights when the stars fell closer to the earth, and every breath released clouds of steam into the brittle air, friends of mine in Cambridge held a party to celebrate Groundhog Day, an annual event for them. I went bundled in an antique fur-lined overcoat with a karakul collar I had inherited from my father, perhaps the only garment I owned that would keep the Boston wind chill at bay. I walked to the house through the cracked-ice streets, slipping and skidding and holding the high, warm collar tight around my neck.

The house was large and well lit and warm, and the party was in full swing by the time I got there. There was a crackling fire in the fireplace and the smell of mulled wine and perfume, and a fine-boned drunken woman in a skewed tiara was singing torch songs at the piano. The soirée went on and on, so late that rather than bear the arrow darts of wind and ice and the long drive home, I decided to stay.

The next day, after a late and full breakfast, a group of us decided to make a pilgrimage to Franklin Park. One of the guests who had stayed over had grown up in old Boston and used to go to the park regularly with her mother back in the 1950s. She had fond memories of the place and was anxious to visit it, even though this was probably not the best day to undertake such an expedition, and she had been forewarned that the park was not what it used to be.

The temperature had plummeted to the single digits, and although still un-iced, the Charles River was sparking with whitecaps in the high winds. But we wrapped ourselves in scarves and borrowed hats, drove over to the park along the Fenway, and made our way to the walking trails around a section of the park called the Wilderness.

The so-called Wilderness is a generally undeveloped section of Franklin Park, intended to give the sense of what the area was like before the Europeans arrived. In fact, it is a recreated wilderness of native trees, such as hickory and hemlock and oak, but nowadays, like so much of New England's native forests, it has been intruded upon by nonnative plants. Not that we cared at this point. Our troop—nine or ten of us—were led on a forced march by our expedition guide, who was determined to get to one of the spots she had known and loved as a child—a flight of steps constructed of Roxbury puddingstone that led to the highest point in the park.

Our leader was a sandy-haired woman with Puritan features named Mary, who dressed in a dark wool overcoat, a trilby hat, and a multitude of scarves. She told us she had been banished to the West Coast at the age of eighteen and had only returned to Boston earlier that year to escape an ex-husband and the tedious fads of shallow California. She seemed also to have the old Puritan tolerance for cold and hardship, and under her governance we marched on, the wind biting at our cheeks, and eventually found the place. For some reason, that day the trail to the heights was cordoned off.

Mary eyed the spot like a general.

"This is meaningless," she announced and ducked under the yellow ribbons and led us upward.

Beyond lay the winter landscape of Franklin Park, any of its rumored unpleasantness obscured by the tree canopy and its pleasure grounds, meadowlands, ponds, and rolling hills stretching out to all quarters of the developed city, an island in urbanity.

But windy. The air on this height was so chipped and iced not one of us could stand it, and we retreated.

"On to the zoo," said Mary.

Franklin Park was considered the jewel in the crown of Frederick Law Olmsted's chain of parks, which began at the Common, swept down along Commonwealth Avenue, and then, from the riverbank at Charlesgate, was supposed to curve all the way around the core of the city in a great green arch from the river, south, southeast to Dorchester Bay, and out to Castle Island on the east. In fact, in Olmsted's time the project never reached the shore, and the greenway more or less ended at Franklin Park, about six miles from the Common.

The 527-acre park, with its woodlands, ponds, statuary, rose gardens, and zoo, was originally laid out in the style of a country park, a design that was popular back in mother England. Olmsted, like Bulfinch before him, had traveled in England and had visited many of the great estates laid out by the eighteenth-century garden and grounds designer Capability Brown, who favored wide vistas backed by woodlands and long central allées, with a distant focal point to draw the eye to the horizon. Brown's idea was to create an idealized version of nature itself, without ornament, unlike the earlier Italianate Renaissance gardens, which were designed, generally speaking, to offset and humanize the natural world. Olmsted, along with an American landscape designer named Andrew Jackson Downing, brought over the ideas of Capability Brown and altered them.

This was a period in American history when the salutary effects of fresh air and exercise were coming into vogue. Bostonians were walking more, bicycles had just become the rage, tennis was popular, as well as rowing and cross-country hiking. With his park designs, Olmsted hoped to encourage these activities and also make them accessible to the poor, of which there were many in Boston by the mid-nineteenth century.

The idea for a ring of green spaces around the city of Boston was launched in the 1870s, part of a vast restoration and regreening project that the city had started in the early decades of the century. It could be argued that the parks movement in the city, and in fact the whole idea of preserving public open space in America, had begun in 1630 when the Puritans purchased, for the sum of thirty pounds, the fifty-acre Common from William Blackstone.

In those first years, the Common was in fact the backside of the town center and was no different from the common pastures of England and Europe, a public holding where citizens of the village could graze their sheep and cows. In Boston, as in Europe, these uses were theoretically regulated so as not to despoil the lands; there was a hired shepherd and cattle herder, the number of cows or sheep that could be grazed there was restricted, and no one was permitted to cut trees.

In spite of the fact that the Boston Common was intended for sheep and cows and also used as a military training ground, the public often walked there to take the air, and in 1675 walkways were laid out around the green, and trees were planted. Here on summer evenings the young sports of the new town strolled with their "Marmalate Madames," as one early British visitor, John Josselyn, pointed out. There were originally three ponds on the Common, two of them since filled, and the third, the Frog Pond, underlain now by concrete. By the nineteenth century the Common was such a popular gathering place that the town fathers began to lay out more tree-lined promenades along the periphery. They moved the gallows to the South End, and in the 1830s, for the benefit of the people, banned cows altogether, planted more than six hundred trees, and constructed fountains and statuary. Then in the 1840s, after some dispute, the little cove known as Round Marsh at the base of the Common, once a popular clamming flat until it was polluted by the increasing populace, was filled and replaced with the Public Garden.

The creation of a purely ornamental planting ground in order to cultivate such useless and decorative elements as flowers would have been contrary to the beliefs of the founders of the city. But the customs of the town were changing, and the restoration of that which the Puritans and subsequent settlers had despoiled was about to begin.

Apart from the original Common, the conscious move toward the creation and preservation of green space in the city had started in 1831 when the 783-acre peninsula began to require open space to bury its dead. The old, unadorned burying grounds, the Granary and Copp's Hill, may have served as grim, conveniently located reminders of the presence of long-legged death favored by the Puritan mind. But there was not enough room for the newly dead, and in the early years of the nineteenth century, innovations in cemetery designs were coming out of Paris, notably the new cemetery at Père Lachaise. In Boston a committee was formed to find a new site for a burial ground ultimately selected a forested tract of approximately one hundred acres just across the Charles in Cambridge. Known locally as Sweet Auburn, the land there was characterized by several steep hills and low bottomlands, wherein grew swampy forests of red maples as well as hilly slopes of chestnuts and oaks. It was a favorite spot for local hunters and also for local bird watchers. One of the great ornithologists of the late nineteenth century, William Brewster, grew up on nearby Brattle Street and used to include Sweet Auburn in his bird-watching rounds. The whole western end of Cambridge was rural in those decades, with hayfields, orchards, ponds, marshes, and a few sections of as yet uncut forest, such as Sweet Auburn.

The Garden and Cemetery Committee planned a landscaped burying ground for Sweet Auburn based on the designs of Père Lachaise. Ultimately they left much of the native forest intact and thereby preserved, almost incidentally, one of the birding meccas of the Boston region. Brewster and students from Harvard, as well as early naturalists such as Thomas Nuttall, had already assembled thorough records of the bird life in the tract, and as the city of Cambridge spread westward and overwhelmed the fields and orchards, Mount Auburn Cemetery, as it was subsequently named, endured as a remnant of the region's primal nature, and served to attract a wide diversity of migratory and local nesting birds.

In 1841 the city purchased a seventy-two-acre parcel of land to create a similarly landscaped burying ground at Forest Hills, in what was then the suburb of Roxbury. Once again trees were planted, statuary was commissioned, and walkways were laid out. The idea was to provide a pleasant place for the dead to repose while at the same time offering a pleasing and soothing landscape of flowering trees and shrubs and wooded glens for the living. As the city spread, the green glades and ponds of Forest Hills also became a haven for wildlife, which by midcentury was increasingly crowded out by the spread of the human population beyond the Shawmut.

By the early 1800s, the population of Boston had grown to 58,000, and by 1850, because of the failure of the potato crop and the onset of Irish immigration, to 180,000. Immigration and the city's tendency to annex nearby towns not only expanded the city population but helped foster a rich new ethnic mix. By the 1870s the population had jumped to over 250,000, and it jumped again by the 1890s to well over 500,000. The African American community, which was as old and original as the Puritan population, increased substantially after the Civil War, driven by the hope of Boston's generally liberal attitude toward blacks (compared to the rest of the United States, at least). Rumors of a "Negro Paradise" in Boston had spread through the rural South, and new immigrants flooded in after the war.

Over in the North End, the old Yankee merchants were replaced by southern Europeans and Irish, and in the West End, Jews, Poles, Irish, Greeks, Portuguese, French Canadians, and anyone else who was not Yankee born and bred crowded together in narrow, dark-streeted slums. The Shawmut was spilling over its boundaries, the poor were crowded together in unwholesome warrens, sewage disposal was primitive, and the omnipresent horse droppings, the nineteenth century's version of automobile exhaust, collected on the city streets in some sections, attracting flies and, incidentally, increasing the population of the newly introduced English sparrow.

The great back bay of the Charles River on the southwest side of the peninsula had become a nauseating waste, so foul and squalid that screeds appeared regularly in the city periodicals, clamoring to have something done to solve the problem. And so the town fathers, following the old Boston tradition, decided to cover up the problem.

This decision begat a thirty-year project that ultimately created 450 acres of new land known as the Back Bay, which expanded the city's dry land by nearly 60 percent. A wide boulevard, *à la Parisienne,* was constructed, with a tree-lined, one-hundred-foot-wide mall down the center, and handsome French Empire dwellings lining the street on either side.

A similar experiment, complete with the by now commonplace filling of swampland, had taken place a few years earlier in the South End, but only a few of the so-called Proper Bostonians settled there. Dentists and nouveaux riches businessmen began to move in—and then out again as it became clear that the new neighborhood was not *the* place to live. By the end of the nineteenth century, the South End had declined into a slum of flophouses, taverns, and cheap restaurants, although these operations were all housed in fine French Empire mansions.

Not so along the newly created Commonwealth Avenue in the Back Bay. The address became as fashionable as Beacon Hill. Nevertheless, the little problem of the rank air of the Charles River flats had not been entirely solved; it had just been moved a little farther out into the river and had been exacerbated by the construction of a commercial dam, plus the presence of warehouses, wharves, and slaughterhouses on the other side of the river. Once again, the answer was to fill it in.

From New York City, the man who had more or less created the field of landscape architecture in America, Frederick Law Olmsted, had been watching the developments in Boston with interest. In 1857 he and the English garden designer Calvert Vaux had won the coveted contract to create Central Park, and the project had been such a success that Olmsted became one of the most sought-after park designers in the country. He was responsible for Prospect Park in Brooklyn, Mount Royal in Montreal, a huge interconnecting park system in Buffalo, New York, parks in Chicago and Milwaukee, and many private estates, such as the immense Biltmore in Asheville, North Carolina. But it was Boston that he was most interested in, and in 1878 he was invited to undertake the Charles River project. The result was the creation of what became one of the best-known and most ambitious urban parks in the United States.

Olmsted solved the sewage problem by creating a floodgate where the marshes of the Muddy River met the Charles, the foulest section of this befouled river. He constructed a series of landscaped holding ponds to store excess water during heavy rains, then rerouted the courses of Stony Brook and the Muddy River, the two waterways that ran down to the Charles, so that they wound through landscaped grounds in sinuous curves, handsomely bridged in stone at certain points along the way.

It was all basically an engineered water drainage system that at once covered over and cleaned the fetid flats that had so offended the noses of the Back Bay residents. What emerged—after some ten years of construction—was an elegant curving greenway, with willows and oaks and maples, walkways, carriageways, and bridle paths; all in all, as Olmsted had wished, it was a picturesque riverine landscape such as he had found in the marshlands, or fens, of eastern England. The park was so named the Back Bay Fens.

By 1890 the green ribbon of the Back Bay Fens that angled up from the Charles was extended to Jamaica Pond. The Muddy River was still a polluted, stagnant, slow-moving stream, lined with garbage dumps and shacks, above the Fens. Olmsted persuaded the cities of Brookline and Boston to work together to improve the flow, reroute the stream, and replant the banks with native trees so that the park would connect with Jamaica Pond, a site upon which the ambitious Olmsted had also set his eyes.

Unlike the river flats and the aptly named Muddy River, Jamaica Pond was clean and had provided drinking water as far back as the eighteenth century, when planners had piped its waters all the way into the center of the old city. The surroundings of the pond, like Sweet Auburn, offered a pleasing rural landscape, with hayfields and a few summer houses. Unlike the huge engineering projects of the Back Bay Fens, all that was necessary at Jamaica Pond was to clear the banks of a few ice-houses and most of the summer houses.

Year by year, decade by decade, the park system was pushing ever southward. And there was more to come.

In 1842 Harvard University was bequeathed a 394-acre estate in Jamaica Plain to be used for an agricultural and horticultural school. After much negotiation, in 1894, Harvard leased the tract to the city to create a public arboretum—the first in the United States, perhaps needless to say, inasmuch as this was Boston. The designer of the grounds—also perhaps needless to say—was Frederick Law Olmsted.

The Arnold Arboretum is still one of the foremost arboretums in the country. Through the ingenuity of its plantings, it provides interest throughout the year, starting in spring with the hazels and pussy willows, andromedas, forsythias, shadbush, azaleas, lilacs, flowering quinces, and rhododendrons, and carrying on all through the growing season and well into late autumn until the last flowering of the witch hazels in December. The Arboretum is eye-catching even in the dead of winter, with its groves of conifers and its collection of various trees with exfoliating bark.

Just east of the Arboretum, along what came to be known as the Arborway, lay the landscaped grounds of Forest Hills Cemetery. By the time Olmsted arrived in Boston, this well-landscaped burying ground had come into its own. It was considered, even by the designer of Mount Auburn, to be a better example of a landscaped country cemetery, a fashion that was by then spreading throughout the nation. Forest Hills was laid out with huge collections of native trees planted around a small lake, including beeches, oaks, lindens, exotic Japanese pines, sequoias, and spruces—nearly 30,000 trees all told—underlain by thickets of rhododendron, azaleas, laurels, and ground covers of ivy and violets.

Olmsted knew of this wooded cemetery and had visited it even before he laid out Central Park. In fact, the landscape of Forest Hills is said to have inspired some of his ideas for the New York project.

Beyond Forest Hills lay yet another tract of open land that was being considered by the city as a possible green space. It was here, starting in 1886, that Olmsted began work on Franklin Park, which he hoped would rival his own Central Park in New York.

Many landscape architects consider the resulting work to be Olmsted's best design. But, as with so many urban projects, many conflicting agencies were vying for use of the property, including those that wanted more active recreational facilities such as ball fields, croquet pitches, tennis courts, and later a golf course—not the sort of rural country park that Olmsted had in mind. Nonetheless, the huge tract of wooded hills and meadows, the unique outcroppings of Roxbury puddingstone, the scenic pond, and the drives and lanes and walking trails combined to create one of the finest urban green spaces in the United States. The only problem was that, unlike Central Park, which is now surrounded by some of the highest-priced real estate in the world, by the 1950s Franklin Park was surrounded by what more affluent residents of the city believed to be, putting it mildly, a depressed neighborhood.

Over the next decade the whole park devolved into a wasteland littered with trash and abandoned cars. The bridges and the flights of stone steps were cracked and uncared for by the responsible city agencies, the greenswards rutted with car tracks. Worst of all, in the eyes of the local populace, the park was a haven for dangerous criminals and drug dealers.

In fact, the park was much safer than the surrounding streets, and decidedly safer than Central Park, but the citizenry thought Franklin Park was dangerous, so no one would go there, and because no one cared, year by year the situation only grew worse, until the park more or less dropped out of the public consciousness.

Finally, in the early 1980s, as a result of the efforts of a single-minded neighbor named Richard Heath, a group was organized to improve the park. Heath and his allies managed to form a partnership with the city to create an annual maintenance contract that would be supplemented by contributions of members of the Friends of Franklin Park and the local business community. Slowly, the grounds began to recover and to draw more visitors. The local neighborhood people started the process, and then, as the neighborhood changed, more and more city residents returned. You see them there on warm days in three seasons of the year, runners and walkers, older people strolling along, deep in conversation, the litter generally cleared away, and a few old men reading the paper in the sun.

Mary was determined to carry on to the zoo, but by this time there arose a mutiny and general desertion of our band, and only five of us dared to press on through the frozen wilderness to the zoo itself.

In spite of recent improvements, much of Franklin Park was a sad remnant of what our guide remembered—although, as she herself admitted, childhood memories can obscure unpleasant details. She had in mind a rose garden, statues of animals, the lions of the zoo, the high peak of the Wilderness as a veritable mountain, prancing dogs, and older couples walking arm in arm on Sunday afternoons.

Whatever landscaped plots we came across that day were weed-choked, and the wind had flipped over garbage cans in some areas, strewing papers and cans across the ground. We saw a dead car at the edge of one roadway, and on another path we came upon a madman. He was dressed lightly for the weather, clad only in a hooded sweatshirt, jeans, and a watch cap, and in order to escape the cold he had transformed himself into a bird and was migrating south. At least that was the only logical explanation we could assume, given his behavior. We saw him approaching from a distance, his arms rising and falling in slow wingbeats, occasionally holding stiff as he soared, his head tipped, from one side of the road to the other, only to resume his slow flapping. He flew by us without a nod, his eyes intent on his personal horizon, as we respectfully stepped aside so as not to disrupt his migration.

We crossed the park and came finally upon the confines of the sad winter zoo. Most of the buildings were closed, and only a few zebras and antelopes grazed in these northern savannas, pawing through the light snow like caribou or bison. Not the best day to visit.

One of the compromises Olmsted agreed to was the placement of a zoological garden in the park. But the actual construction was not completed until 1913, when the zoo finally opened to the public. Like Franklin Park itself, the zoo has had its ups and downs. For a while when it first opened, when the park was still a pleasure ground, the Boston populace would gather there on Sunday afternoons; attendance was free, and as many as 2 million people a year paid a visit over the subsequent decades. Then, in the 1950s, the city started charging admission, and attendance declined, funding dropped, and the animal exhibits dwindled to a few sad lions and the like. But with the restoration of the park in the 1980s, the zoo also improved. A children's section was established, a tropical aviary was built, and, more importantly, an educational element was added that attempted to link the exhibits to international wildlife conservation issues.

The zoo, of course, is populated with exotic, nonnative species, lions and snow leopards, rare forest antelopes, rare wild African dogs, rare tropical birds, tapirs and capybaras, kangaroos, giraffes and zebras. Also gorillas. One of these, a popular attraction named Joe, made a break for freedom one summer day. He scaled a tall fence and made his way through the park to a bus stop, where he paused, unintentionally terrorizing the innocent passengers. But these creatures are not the only exotic animals. As the plantings in Olmsted's park system began to grow, animals not seen in the confines of Boston for more than one hundred years began to return.

The late-nineteenth-century period of park building and preservation efforts was not limited to Boston. Agriculture in New England had been in sharp decline ever since the opening of the Middlesex Canal in 1825, which permitted the importation of wheat from the rich croplands of upstate New York. The landscape and land use of the whole Northeast was changing. Urban dwellers, including influential citizens such as

William Brewster of Cambridge, were lamenting the loss of farmland and woodlots to the expanding trolley-car suburbs that were spidering out of the central city and overtaking the countryside. The abandonment of farms meant that in those areas not yet consumed by housing and roads, the forest slowly began to return to the outskirts of the city.

In the first few decades of the nineteenth century, the local farmers did not linger when they left. Some simply packed what they could in their wagons, closed the old front door without locking, and pushed off. Roof lines sagged, windows were blown in by winter storms, swallows and raccoons took over, and in the vegetable plots and hayfields beyond, gray birch and dogwood and other sun-loving trees began to spread. These gave way slowly to maple and oak, hickory and ash, and the quintessential tree of northeastern New England, the white pine. The old forest that had grown up some 8,000 years ago, after the retreat of the ice, had been waiting in the deep soil banks over the 250 years of English agricultural practices, and now that plowed lands had been left to their own devices, the seeds sprouted and the forest came back.

In the mid-nineteenth century, something like 85 percent of New England was farmland and field. By the middle of the twentieth century, the statistic was reversed, and the reforestation has continued into our time. There is now more forest in New England than anywhere else in the United States other than the Pacific Northwest.

With the return of the forest, the wildlife species that had been extirpated by the early colonists began to creep back. First the white-tailed deer, then the beaver, then the fox and the bear, the fisher and wild turkey and then, finally, that old demon of the Puritan wilderness, the wolf, or whatever it was that stalked the colonial landscape—wolf or eastern coyote.

Over the decades in the older suburbs, the trees and shrubs of the backyards matured, providing accidental corridors of wild land, used at night by the foxes and coyotes and raccoons and possums. The forest cover increased to such an extent that the returning natives began to make their way even into Boston itself. Here, in the great chain of Olmsted's parks that circled the inner city, they found suitable habitats.

In the mid-1980s, neighbors spotted a strange mammal near Jamaica Pond. About the size of a cat, it had a long narrow face and a sharp snout, with a row of nasty, sharp teeth and a long, thick tail. Inasmuch as most of the people living around Jamaica Pond at that time had come either from other parts of the city or from the well-protected suburbs of the nation, no one in the vicinity had seen such a beast. It was later identified as a fisher, a large weasel-like animal that had been extirpated from the Shawmut as early as the late seventeenth century.

On an autumn day at about the same time, a moose made its way into a fenced backyard in nearby Natick. White-tailed deer were spotted within Boston's city limits, and residents of Brookline reported a strange wild dog with a triangular face and a brushy tail, later determined to be a coyote. Turkeys moved in. One morning in Brookline a powerful male, its tail outspread, chased an innocent commuter away from his car, which was parked in his own driveway. Small flocks of turkeys were seen scratching in the gardens of Newton. Turkeys moved into Franklin Park, turkey vultures sailed over the city, red-tailed hawks began nesting on cornices near the Athenaeum, Boston's august independent library and museum, and, in one of the most remarkable returns, the formerly endangered peregrine falcons (with a little help from restoration programs) began nesting on various high office buildings around the financial district. They fed well on the starlings and pigeons of the nearby parks.

Boston is not exactly overrun with wildlife, unless you count the rats and pigeons and the vast, milling numbers of primates that have settled here, but in our time there is, or seems to be so far, a sort of détente between the resident primates with all their vainglorious self-importance, and what we, the primates, have termed lesser species.

Along with the former native New England species, there also came into Boston in the twentieth century a number of birds and mammals that had never before been found in this region. In the 1950s a ratlike creature with a naked tail and a sharp nose came into town. Native Americans from areas south of New England knew this species well, as did African Americans who had moved up to Boston from the rural South. The Indians called it *umpossum,* transliterated to English as opossum and then later shortened to possum. The red fox, which some biologists believe is a more southern species, moved into the region, as did the gray fox, also considered to be from farther south. Even the common cottontail rabbit may have replaced a more northern New England species, according to some biologists.

New birds appeared as well. First the cardinal, sometime in the 1950s, then the tufted titmouse and the mockingbird and, more recently, the Carolina wren, the turkey vulture, and the red-headed woodpecker, all southern species, and all following, some believe, the warming patterns of global climate change.

From the zoo, the leader of our chilled little entourage decided to make an overland trek through the park straight back to our cars, which we had left near the Forest Hills entrance. This involved a certain amount of bushwhacking through thickets and frozen wet spots and along allées of old oaks and maples. Everywhere in the light snow cover there were tracks. Here the single line of a fox, there the sprawled and scattered rambles of a coyote, or perhaps a dog, and in many spots the carefully placed paw prints of feral cats, who, along with the wild natives, have taken up residence in the Wilderness of Franklin Park. Accompanying the little basting stitches of white-footed mouse tracks and the leaping sets of squirrel tracks, we saw scrapes where some unidentified beast had pawed the snow to get to ground cover below, probably a white-tailed deer. And periodically, in out-of-the-way spots, we came across the footprints of errant couples out on some obscure mission about which we dared not speculate.

Franklin Park is hardly a small pocket wilderness, nor is it linear. It's a great sprawling tract, cut through with roads and walkways here and there, none of which is marked when you happen upon one midstream, so to speak. We had no map with us and were navigating by blind reckoning and memory, and in due time we determined that we were lost. There were no landmarks that we recognized, nothing to go by but the sun, which was by then sinking in the west. But having come in from the west, we carried on toward the setting sun, presuming we would strike a road eventually.

At one point in our trek we came to a site that Mary claimed she recognized, although, she said, it had been much improved since her childhood. This was, she believed, the place called Schoolmaster Hill. At her insistence we ascended to have a look around. We could see the distant towers of the city to the north and the open stretches of the golf course, and the forested rises and the low hills to the west, where we were headed.

The hill was named for Ralph Waldo Emerson, who lived in a rented house at this location for two years, starting in 1823, while he was teaching school in nearby Roxbury. He loved the view from this spot, which in some ways, thanks to Olmsted, is probably not that much altered from the time when Emerson lived here. Even in the mid-nineteenth century it was wooded with ancient trees and presented a "sylvan" (as Emerson wrote) landscape, rare in his day. You can still see over to Olmsted's Sheep Meadow, which in 1915 was turned into a golf course, but which retains, albeit without grazing flocks, a rolling, open greensward. You can also see over to Great Blue Hill, the highest peak in this region of (former) peaks and hills.

On other outings, and in far better weather, I have taken a drink on the terrace of the golf course—not because I would dare to entertain myself in so idle and un-Puritanical a sport as golf, but because in my opinion the site offers one of the finest vistas in all of Boston, if you know what you're looking at. From the terrace the course rolls out in a series of gently undulating hills and dales to a distant wooded horizon. Trees form a bank on either side of the meadow, gently guiding the eye outward and upward to the western sky. None of this is accident; it was carefully planned by Frederick Law Olmsted, and it has all the elements of the Arcadian ideal that was so much a part of Capability Brown's landscapes and of Olmsted's work. With a little imagination, if you can block out the golfers and the comings and goings on the terrace, you could be on one of the great estates of England, Madingley Hall or Castle Ashby or of any of the other 170 or so estates and country gardens laid out by Capability Brown and his associates. Better yet, you could be in the idealized landscape of Arcadia, with open meads and, beyond—charged with the possibility of nymphs and satyrs and even that old demon Pan—thickets of forest, springs, pools, and outcroppings of ancient rocks. As it is, it's hard to believe, when conditions are right, that you are no more than a few hundred yards from the mean streets of a crowded city on the eastern seaboard of North America.

Emerson was inspired by the same feeling in his little aerie on the hill. As he wrote, there was no woodland as fine as this within a hundred miles. "When I am safe in my sylvan home," he wrote, "I tread on the pride of Greece and Rome."

From our perch on Schoolmaster Hill, we could get a fix on the general position of our cars and we set out once more, this time following paths, which although still unmarked, seemed to lead us in the proper direction. We trekked onward and found ourselves on a wide paved road, which we followed until we saw a narrower trail leading off in the proper direction, and in time we came out on Forest Hills Street and made our way back to our cars.

We were all chilled, but no one was frostbitten, and we proceeded to an Irish pub on Centre Street to drink hot whiskey and reminisce.

The school where Emerson was teaching in 1823 and Franklin Park itself were not far from the site of the transcendentalist and socialist experimental community known as Brook Farm, which was organized by George Ripley in 1841. Ripley consulted with Emerson before organizing the commune, and one of the Concord authors, Nathaniel Hawthorne, was a trustee and lived there for a while. The experiment was well known to Bronson Alcott, Margaret Fuller, Elizabeth Peabody, and many other luminaries of the great literary flowering going on in Boston and Concord at the time. Interestingly enough, the more independent transcendentalists such as Henry Thoreau and Ralph Waldo Emerson never joined.

Emerson, with his views on self-reliance and nature, was almost a demigod among Bostonians of the proper sort. Instead of reciting grace before dinner, certain family patriarchs would read extended passages from his work. The large funeral of Ralph Forbes, the head of one of the most august Brahmin families, included a very short reading from the Bible and a very long reading from Emerson. Thoreau, in his time and for many decades after, was not as popular as he is today. But the ideas of these two Concordians—both of whom were children of Harvard University, the sort of educational institution that was de rigueur for the Bostonians who were reading Emerson and Thoreau—had a powerful influence on the public mind. By the 1860s, thanks in part to these two, and also to the great landscape painters of the Hudson River School, such as Thomas Cole and Frederick Church, American attitudes toward nature and even that old abomination of the Puritan mind, wilderness itself, was softening.

Boston Common, the first publicly financed open space in

the new American colony, was purchased from Blackstone for pragmatic reasons: the locals needed a cow common. But other communities bought land for other purposes. In 1853 the Laurel Hill Association in Stockbridge, Massachusetts, saved over three hundred acres of forest to improve and preserve the natural character of the village—not because they needed the wood but for aesthetic reasons. By the time of the Civil War, the preservation of large tracts of wilderness had become a national campaign—although supported mainly by easterners. In 1872 an immense tract of wilderness known as the Yellowstone, complete with hot springs and geysers, was purchased by the federal government and set aside as what was termed a "national park"—the first such open space in the world. Other huge national parks followed, including the controversial and hard-won Yosemite Valley, which, like all the others, was preserved for aesthetic, even spiritual, reasons.

In these hopeful fin de siècle decades, well-to-do families would retreat to the North Woods of Maine and the Adirondacks to live rough in makeshift camps and spend their days hunting or fishing or climbing and their nights lounging by the fireside, listening to the eerie moans and howls emanating from the night forest and the tall tales told to the credulous urbanites by their forest guides, who knew just what kind of story to tell.

All this outdoor activity for no particular purpose was primarily a diversion of the eastern mind. Out in the West, Americans were still in the process of subduing the land. Bounty hunters worked dutifully to clear the last of the big predators, the wolf and the cougar, and, while they were at it, the innocent buffalo, whose herds had once moved like a dark tide across the Plains. The pioneers had long since cleared the midwestern skies of the passenger pigeons, and while easterners were battling to save wilderness, in the West the land was still being cleared of forest and wild prairie, wild beasts, and also that company of Bradford's "wilder men"—the Indians.

Even as the slaughter of animals continued in the West, here in the East, in a subtler way, the carnage was still taking place. The menus for Lock-Ober and other fashionable Boston restaurants still offered rare or endangered shore birds and ducks. A new hobby involving the collection of bird eggs was in fashion; immigrants from southern Europe were hunting songbirds on weekends throughout the year; and on the streets of Boston and New York, and in fact all across the country, women were promenading in hats decorated with the nuptial plumes of egrets and herons, the acquisition of which was causing the demise of some 5 million plume birds a year.

In the same period, however, Bostonians were taking up another interesting hobby. In their free time, both men and women would ride the trolleys out to the end of the line and head to the woods and fields or wander through the newly created parks with opera glasses or field glasses in order to look—not shoot, mind you, just look—at the resident and migratory birds. In spite of their continuing taste for snipe and curlew, Bostonians seemed to be developing a genuine appreciation for bird life.

The appreciation may have been there for generations. John James Audubon came to the city in 1832 with prints from his monumental *Birds of America* and sold nine subscriptions for the work in the first week, more than he had sold in any other city he had visited. The Athenaeum, one of the earliest independent libraries in the Americas, mounted an exhibition of his drawings, and according to Audubon, the outpouring of kindness he received in the city exceeded that of any other place. Among other prominent Bostonians, he was introduced to the well-known Harvard botanist Thomas Nuttall, and the two men went off searching for birds around the newly created Mount Auburn Cemetery. Audubon collected an olive-sided flycatcher that day, an as yet undescribed species that Nuttall had first identified.

Nuttall was an English naturalist who had written the first field guide to American birds and had traveled widely in the South and West on collecting trips. In the early decades of the nineteenth century, he voyaged up the Missouri River, covering some of the same territory, more or less, that Lewis and Clark had passed through. He collected many plants as yet unknown to science on the expedition, which he sent back to the botanical garden of Liverpool. In 1818 he published his *Genera of North American Plants,* and in 1822 he was hired as curator of the botanical garden at Harvard, then located in Cambridge. (The Arnold Arboretum was yet to come.)

During his wide-ranging voyages around North America, Nuttall ended up in San Diego, California. Here he met up with another widely traveled Bostonian, Richard Henry Dana, the author and sailor for whom my brother named his reborn vessel. Nuttall even had a walk-on part in Dana's monumental work, *Two Years Before the Mast.*

Young Richard Henry Dana, who was all of nineteen when he left Boston, had known Nuttall at Harvard. Dana sailed from Boston as a seaman on the trading vessel the *Pilgrim,* which rounded Cape Horn and anchored off San Diego to take on cattle hides. One day on the beach there, Dana saw an old man in a sailor's pea jacket and a straw hat, his trousers rolled, picking up shells and stones and other curiosities. It turned out to be Nuttall. He had left Boston about the same time as the *Pilgrim* and had traveled overland to the Pacific Northwest. Now he was making his way south on the California coast, examining trees and shrubbery and birds along the way. He had heard there was a ship outbound for Boston and had come to San Diego to book passage aboard the *Pilgrim*. The sailors thought him a bit daft because of his intense interest in shells and plants and birds and anything else he had never seen before. He was dubbed "Old Curious" by the crew.

Boston adopted the new fashion of bird watching with a passion. The pursuit was an acceptable entertainment for both men and women, and a gentleman could take up the sport without casting doubt upon his masculinity; in fact many of the most active birders were also hunters. William Brewster himself, who is considered one of the most important figures in American ornithology, was a duck hunter and even supported the rights of the market gunners.

One of the quintessential Proper Bostonians, J. P. Marquand's fictionalized character George Apley, took up the art of weekend bird watching. He and a lady friend would go out in the fields around Brookline on a Saturday morning making lists of the birds they spotted. It is generally accepted that Apley was based on the very real personage of Ralph Forbes, the man who requested an extended reading of Emerson at his funeral. But other nonfictional Proper Bostonians were active bird watchers. Brewster, of course, was prime among these, but so also was Harold Bowditch, a relative of Nathaniel Bowditch, the father of modern maritime navigation, as were Reginald

Heber Howe and Dr. Windsor Tyler, who became an authority on bird song.

A popular birding spot just over the Boston line in Brookline was known as Hall's Pond. This small body of water, only a few blocks from Coolidge Corner, was named for the family who owned the land around the pond, and one of the most active birders in the area was a woman named Minna Hall. She was well known in Boston social circles, a regular at the Friday afternoon subscription concerts of the Boston Symphony, a regular attendee of luncheons at the Chilton Club, and also, as one of her friends suggested, a gadabout. Minna lived for a very long time, as so many Boston women did; at age ninety she was still said to be doing too much gadding about.

Minna had a cousin named Harriet Hemenway, who was also a gadabout, a powerful figure in Boston circles, and a serious bird watcher. She and Minna, like so many in their clique, would go out on weekend bird walks. The two cousins often circled Hall's Pond in suitable weather. One day there in 1896, Harriet related the details of a horrific story she had read about the slaughter of egrets, herons, and terns for their nuptial plumes, which were used to adorn the immense, elaborate hats of women of the day. Minna was properly outraged.

It should be said that Boston women such as Harriet Hemenway and Minna Hall were never slaves to fashion. Known among certain social circles in less enlightened cities as "low heelers," they tended to dress in high-collared black crêpe, with an understated pearl choker, and wore their hair in the Queen Mother style with impunity. The fashion seemed to be a statement of a certain position in society, an expression of "to the manner born," so to speak. Ever since Katherine Nanny Naylor exhibited the audacity to sue her well-connected husband for divorce (and to win, no less), Boston seems to have bred up an intensely powerful class of women activists, such as Abigail Adams and a host of others through the centuries. In the late nineteenth century, women even managed, contrary to all upright Victorian sensibilities, to establish the unique institution known as the Boston marriage, in which two women lived together in seeming marital harmony. They could acceptably travel abroad together and attend dinner parties and symphony and luncheons at the Chilton Club as a couple. No one seems to have questioned these relationships, although one has to wonder what was whispered around the fires at the Boston men's clubs.

Hemenway and Hall were indignant over the frivolity that was generating the slaughter of plume birds, and so, inasmuch as they were Boston women and not given to complacency or silence or indifference in the face of cruelty, they decided to do something.

Another institution that had established itself in Boston, was, even into the late 1880s, taking its cue from Mother Britain: the tradition of afternoon tea. As the sometime Boston-associated author Henry James wrote in *The Portrait of a Lady,* there was nothing quite so fine, in a civilized sort of way, as the taking of afternoon tea, although in the rarefied atmosphere of Beacon Hill the ritual was a subdued affair: an open house, a silver service, lapsang souchong tea, accompanied by simple fare—nothing more elaborate than buttered toast in many parlors. But tea, like coffee, was the stuff of revolution.

The two cousins pored over the Blue Book, the veritable bible of Boston society, and made a list of friends and allies whom they thought might support their idea. Then they held a series of teas. And at these quiet little gatherings, they described the slaughter of the birds, the decimation of the once vast populations, the young left starving in their nests, and encouraged the ladies to sign a pledge never to buy a plumed hat again. Within a few weeks they had nine hundred members, consisting of women from some of the more powerful families around Boston—the Cabots and Lowells and Saltonstalls, Adamses and Wigglesworths, Higginsons and Forbeses. Wisely, Hemenway and Hall also contacted men in the local Boston scientific community and encouraged them to join. Soon the idea was expanding, and the new organization, which had voted to call itself the Massachusetts Audubon Society, began to spread the word to other states, encouraging them to create similar organizations. They even got up a fund to help finance new groups.

In effect this was a boycott, a device sometimes used by their socialist adversaries. But Boston being Boston, it was an acceptable strategy. After all, the city had had a similarly successful political tea party back in the eighteenth century. And in any case, both Harriet and Minna believed in the tradition of noblesse oblige. For a while Harriet had lived with her own mother in a settlement house for unwed mothers. Harriet Hemenway had even mildly shocked the generally tolerant city by inviting a black man to spend the night in her house on Clarendon Street while he was visiting Boston. Never mind that he was Booker T. Washington, a favored Negro among liberal-minded whites in the sometimes rough struggle for freedom that was just beginning and was centered in Boston at the time.

Boston women were not politically naïve. They were quite aware of the fact that they did not have a voice in the congress of men, so Hemenway and Hall determined to elect a gentleman as president of their little organization. They knew just where to look: across the river on Brattle Street, to the home of William Brewster. By 1896 Brewster was one of the best-known names in the birding world, and with him as their head the new society would gain national recognition—which is what the women wanted. This was, after all, a national issue; plumed hats were all the rage throughout the United States.

Brewster had grown up on Brattle Street, a short walk from the river, the gentle hills of Sweet Auburn, and the long fields and open pastures and marshes that surrounded Fresh Pond. From early childhood he was given to rambling, and he and his fellow adventurers explored the local environment, swimming the Charles, hunting, and, later, collecting birds' eggs. His expanding collection of eggs generated an interest in the birds themselves, and he began, like others in his time, to simply observe them. The joy of the hunt was replaced by the joy of pure discovery of new species, and Brewster began keeping field notes and collecting what he determined to be new species for the region. His father, a prosperous banker, held substantial real estate in the Cambridge and Boston area, and it was not necessary for son William to actually work—a state of affairs that many well-off Bostonians of later generations enjoyed. In his youth Brewster had an undiagnosed eye condition and seems to have had trouble reading, so he was educated at home and did not, as was the custom of his class, attend Groton and Harvard. But he was well connected and well known for his observant and accurate field notes, and in spite of his lack of traditional education, he began working in association with the Museum of Comparative Zoology at Harvard, which was founded in 1859 by no less a figure than Louis Agassiz, the father of American science.

Every Monday evening, starting in 1871, when Brewster was twenty years old, he and a group of friends who were also interested in birds used to meet in the attic of Brewster's parents' house on Brattle Street to discuss bird life and peruse a rare treasure owned by the Brewster family, John James Audubon's five-volume *Ornithological Biography*. After two years of meetings, the group expanded and established what they decided to call the Nuttall Club. Ten years later, in 1881, the core group created another organization, the American Ornithologists' Union. Brewster's reputation was widening, and a few years later he was appointed curator of birds at the Harvard Museum.

Inasmuch as they were serious bird watchers and also well connected, Hemenway and Hall wrote to Brewster and asked if he would serve as president of their group. The women's little bird club, which they elected to call the Massachusetts Audubon Society, was strictly a political organization. Its intent was to halt the slaughter of plume birds and also to protect, as an early bulletin pointed out, "our valuable and beautiful wild birds." This was not the kind of work Brewster was known for, but he agreed to serve.

Within the year, the boycott began to work. Massachusetts passed a bill outlawing trade in wild bird plumes, and in 1898 a Massachusetts senator introduced a bill to the U.S. Congress to prohibit both the sale and the shipment of plumes. The bill failed, but the little flame ignited in Boston began to spread. In 1900 Congressman John Lacey of Iowa proposed a bill that prohibited the interstate shipment of animals killed in violation of local state laws. Coupled with strong local bird protection laws, the legislation slowly began to have an effect on the trade. In 1913 a stronger bill was passed, protecting migratory birds altogether, and by 1916 an even stronger law expanded the restrictions in an agreement with Great Britain.

The work of Hemenway and Hall was not over, however. A clause in the original charter stated that the society existed to protect habitats as well as birds. That singular clause set the organization on a course of land acquisition that ultimately resulted in the preservation of some 33,000 acres in the state of Massachusetts. In 1995 one tract acquired by the society, the Boston Nature Center in Mattapan, was reclaimed from the site of an abandoned hospital that included one of Mr. Cooper's community gardens, which the Massachusetts Audubon Society maintained and expanded. The sanctuary has over two miles of trails that wind through meadows and wetlands and provides habitat for local species that have managed to return to the city in recent decades, including the eastern coyote.

Hemenway and Hall's organization was not alone in these efforts. Twenty years earlier one of the hardy Boston adventurers, Edward Pickering, along with twenty-two similarly minded outdoorsmen, banded together to form a hiking club. Most of the mountains they climbed were in the ancient Appalachian range, so the men decided to call their organization the Appalachian Mountain Club. These men were serious climbers. They would travel all around New England, scaling high peaks and camping out on the slopes under the stars. There was nothing outrageous about this in 1876; other prominent Bostonians and New Yorkers were undertaking similar expeditions. But Pickering and his friends began to construct huts along some of the more frequented trails for use by other hikers. Their guiding philosophy was that hiking was in itself a means of spiritual renewal and a way to increase awareness of the beauties of the natural world.

On their treks, however, they had witnessed the destruction of forests taking place because of irresponsible timber practices. Since the club's intent was to promote the protection of mountainscapes as wilderness and to maintain usable trails for other hikers, they felt obligated to build more huts. By 1879 the club had constructed a shelter at Tuckerman's Ravine in the White Mountains, followed by a hut at Madison Spring. Others were built over the following decades, and the club now maintains a range of huts, shelters, and campsites all along the Appalachian Trail, which runs along the ridges of the East Coast from Maine to Georgia.

Another local hiker and rambler—although in tamer environments—was a young protégé of Olmsted's named Charles Eliot. Eliot, whose father would later become president of Harvard, had lived for three years with his family in Europe, where young Charles would visit the old parks and botanical gardens. He was sickly as a child, and in keeping with the wisdom of the times, his father encouraged outdoor activity as a cure. As a result Charles acquired the habit of rambling. He and a friend or two would take a trolley out to the end of the line, then bushwhack cross-country through the woods and fields to the next trolley connection. Eliot would make notes on the flora and fauna during these expeditions, and over the years, he came to know intimately the wilder landscape that lay within a trolley ride of the city. His interest deepened, and after graduation from Harvard in 1882, he became an apprentice to Frederick

Law Olmsted. Five years later, after a trip to Europe, he opened his own landscape design firm.

The creation of the Boston park system had begun as a result of pressure from the public in 1869, but even though Olmsted worked hard to imitate nature, the parks and greens of the city were essentially shaped environments, the work of engineers and landscapers. No one was promoting the idea of preserving whatever undeveloped wild lands still existed in and around Boston. In 1890 Eliot wrote a letter to the popular magazine *Garden and Forest,* in which he proposed the creation of an association that would work to preserve the nearby wild landscapes that he so enjoyed tramping through. He argued that a statewide nonprofit organization should be formed to hold land, free of taxes, for the public. The idea of holding land in trust was, at the time, a unique concept; Eliot's argument was that the organization would maintain landscapes and historic sites in the same way that a library or a museum maintains books and paintings. As was customary, he enlisted his prominent Boston friends, including, among some four hundred others, Charles Sprague Sargent, the director of the Arnold Arboretum; Oliver Wendell Holmes; the historian Francis Parkman; and Olmsted himself. Armed with this sort of backing, it would be hard not to succeed in Boston, and eventually an organization known as the Trustees of Reservations was established. It became the nation's first private statewide preservation group. A few years after its founding, in a reversal of the usual international exchange, in which Boston would follow the British lead, England picked up on the American idea and in 1895 created the National Trust for Places of Historic Interest and Natural Beauty to help preserve its fast-disappearing great estates.

Around Boston, shortly after the group was organized, the Trustees began acquiring land, first Rocky Narrows in Sherborn, then the Lynn Woods and Waverly Oaks. They soon expanded their holdings to include Monument Mountain, in Great Barrington, Nantasket Beach, and other outlying, undeveloped, and scenic areas. By 1900 the Trustees controlled thirteen miles of ocean frontage and about fifty-six miles of riverbank, some 10,000 acres all told. Then in 1903 a state group organized by Eliot, the Metropolitan District Commission, carried on with the idea of park expansion and created a huge swath of green space around the city, starting in the south from the Blue Hills Reservation and circling up to Revere Beach in the north. Currently the Trustees controls over 55,000 acres around the state.

Unfortunately, Charles Eliot did not live to see the full fruition of what had seemed perhaps a wild fantasy of youth; he died in 1897 of spinal meningitis at the age of thirty-eight, at the very height of his success.

All this park building and land preservation around the city had taken place under the rule of the old patrician Anglo-Saxon guard. In the early part of the twentieth century this group was still fixed in its old-school ways: the women gathered at teas and in sewing circles, the men sheltering in their wood-paneled clubs. Formal dances forbade even so tame a display as the fox trot, and the strict social mores still required chaperones in the form of sharp-eyed old doyennes guarding their young virgins from hungry Harvard wolves. Either despite, or perhaps because of, this natural conservatism, it was this same class of people who saved and restored much of the local landscape. Soon, along with allies on the West Coast, such as John Muir, and conservationists from New York City and Philadelphia, a national movement to protect the threatened landscapes of the American environment was born.

Unfortunately, however, less than one hundred years after the movement began, what had been saved in Boston was almost destroyed. By 1950 an energetic group of modernist businessmen and politicians set out to create a new city on the erstwhile hills of the Shawmut, and they were determined to carry out this goal even if it meant destroying the hard-won parks and public gardens and surrounding wild lands in the process.

CHAPTER FIVE

Scoundrel Spring

Decline and Fall in a Green City

I WAS AWAY from the city for a while that winter and returned by air in early March. I had been in Savannah, where the azaleas were just coming into bloom, the tulips and daffodils were making palette dashes of color all through the city squares, and thick vines of wisteria were winding over the arched doorways, hot to blossom.

It was sunny when I left the South, with billowing, summer-like clouds forming over the pinelands of Georgia and South Carolina. But somewhere north of New York I could see a low bank of misty clouds, into which the plane soon descended. And then we were back in gray old Boston, the plane skimming over the rock-bound harbor islands. The whole world had turned to seamless gray. Gray sky, gray seas, gray waters of the harbor, interrupted only by a slim white ribbon of surf against the gray eastern shores of the islands, and the gray, stacked city rising beyond, with gray hills sweeping westward, offset only by patches of white snow. Merely to look upon this scene was to sense an internal chill, the bite of river winds, creeping dismal fogs, and a cold rain drizzling out of the low clouds. I believe it was Mark Twain who claimed that any poets who dared to write about beautiful springs in New England should be shot on sight.

It is possible that local weather, along with the sea, was one of the things that helped shape the character of the true Bostonian. John Winthrop, who was something of a weather watcher and recorded daily meteorological conditions on the peninsula, was fooled in the early years. The first two winters in the new colony were warmer than usual, and as a result Winthrop believed he and his company had landed in a benign environment. But he should have listened to the local Massachusett Indians, who had explained to him that winters in their country were bitter, save that every ten years or so there was no winter at all.

In the third winter of the little colony, the Indians were proved right. The cold snapped down from the Arctic, bringing in relentless sea winds filled with snow and sleet, followed by brilliantly clear, cold days. The harbor froze over, and the ice on the Charles was so thick that horses and carts were able to cross over to the north bank.

In fact, Boston does have an odd mix of weather patterns that tend to induce a certain ambiguity. The Shawmut Peninsula is located in the midst of opposing air currents that swirl in from parts of the globe as far as a thousand miles away, ranging from the Arctic tundra to the southwest, the Gulf of Mexico, and of course, and most often, the North Atlantic.

The English who settled on the Shawmut were particularly struck by the nature of the northwest winds that blew in each winter. Back in England winds rarely came out of the northwest, and the normal winter weather pattern was mostly cool, dank rain or dull, low clouds that would settle in and last for weeks. In New England, winds from the northwest brought cold, sunny periods from the Arctic. In later years the colonists were wise enough to recognize this pattern and develop the classic saltbox design for their houses, with a long sloping roof to the northwest and a short roof in front, the façade facing southeast and banked with windows for solar gain.

In summer the weather systems tend to haul around to the southwest and come up across the continent, bringing warm weather, a fact also well known to the local Indians. The southwest was, in their view, a benign, mythic country where Chi' Manitou, the Great Spirit himself, lived. It was the place where all the Indian spirits would go after they died.

Southeast winds in summer in Boston, which come in over the ocean, can bring fog under certain conditions or heavy rain if they are part of a low-pressure system. In the time of sailing ships, some of these southeasters could be dangerous to coastal shipping and shore installations and could cause flooding. Hurricanes also followed this track, as John Winthrop noted early on. He recorded in his journal the advent of a frightful wind that rose up on an August night in 1635 and uprooted hundreds of trees, destroyed houses, and drove the four-hundred-ton vessel *Great Hope* ashore. Having witnessed this mighty tempest, as well as the region's cold winters, Winthrop changed his mind about the benign nature of Boston and thought it a "sorry climate for living in."

It was the northeast wind that Winthrop and later weather watchers came to dread the most. After having lived a few years on the Shawmut, Winthrop noticed that the east wind would bring in rain or snow, which could be decidedly heavy. Winds from this quarter bore watching in any season, he learned.

They tended to bring fast-moving fogs down on those at sea and created what became known later as backdoor cold fronts, which brought cool air to the coastline. But the worst of the east winds were the dreaded northeast storms that descended upon the port city with a fury and were the undoing of many sturdy Boston-built vessels, from large sailing ships and steamers to the hardy little fishing schooners out on Georges Bank.

New England weather has probably generated more axioms than any other region in the United States, the most famous being "if you don't like the weather, wait a minute." The swirling air patterns that twist over the Shawmut in all seasons of the year mean that whatever weather has arrived will not last very long—three days at most, generally speaking—although I have noticed that in spring a hideous sunless chill from the east can settle in and endure for a week at a time. This is still a short time compared to the world from which the Puritans had come, where the city of London can go for a month without any sun whatsoever. Here in Boston, you just have to wait it out.

As Mark Twain said in a speech delivered to the New England Society in 1876, the weather in New England is always doing something, getting up to new designs and trying them out on people. He claimed to have counted 136 different kinds of weather in a single day, although even more cynical weathermen have since pointed out that Twain was not a meteorologist and had greatly underestimated the situation.

True to form, two days after I got back from Savannah, something changed. The wind shifted out of the northeast and hauled around to the southwest, then carried on to the southeast, and suddenly the temperature began to rise. It was in the forties when I got up, the fifties by the time I finished breakfast, and had reached the mid-sixties with full sun by midmorning. I bundled up nonetheless—knowing what I know about local weather—and set out on an expedition to the Arboretum, to see what the pussy willows were about.

Along the Fenway and the Arborway, packs of joggers were out, trotting along like neighborhood dogs on a mission. Some, as in December, had stripped to shorts and T-shirts and were clearly overheated at that. The willows were greening, and there was a fresh haze of color in the swelling tree buds, and down in the low spots and sinks along the Muddy River, the false hellebores and the skunk cabbages were spearing up out of the moist earth. Spring was in the air. You could smell it everywhere, half dank earth, half floral, and rank with the promise of new life—never mind the automobile exhaust.

For all its grim visage, March in Boston is the season of hope, or at least is supposed to be. Under normal winter conditions—which hardly exist anymore, if they ever did—snow would descend on Boston sometime in November and lie around in open areas until late in March, then melt. The winters were long; some of the worst blizzards in the city, such as the great snowstorm of 1888, have occurred in March. More recently, on March 12, 1993, the so-called storm of the century began, one of the largest storms ever recorded in North America. It battered the entire East with heavy snows and high winds, dumping more snow in one storm than had fallen in the entire winter.

But in the classic lion-and-lamb metaphor that characterizes the month of March, all across the city, in the rolling open glades of Franklin Park, out along the Esplanade and the banks of the Charles, in the few remaining wetlands and the myriad uncounted acres of backyards and vacant lots that survive within the official city limits, the season was stirring. Salamanders, which spend most of their lives underground, emerged to migrate to local ponds and wetlands, where they would mate and laid their eggs. In every available hollow and sink, the little spring peepers began to call. Wherever there were vernal pools, wood frogs were voicing their quacking, ducklike mating croak, and little fairy shrimps—tiny, almost microscopic crustaceans—were drifting in the murky waters.

At the Arboretum little companies of mothers pushing baby carriages were proceeding down Meadow Road, past the katsuras and the redwoods and the horse chestnuts. The red-winged blackbirds, which had not left until December that year, a month later than usual, were back in town. Everywhere along the Arborway I could hear their pleasant broken song, mixed with the chattering of starlings and English sparrows, and also the twittering of house finches, chickadees, the whistles of titmice and cardinals, and the distant hammering of woodpeckers. The robins were back in town, too, some of them having never left that winter. Mockingbirds were singing, and the air was moist and scented with fresh earth. In grassy areas, I could see the holes of worms that had emerged on the wet nights and the little remnants of tunnels of meadow voles, which are active all winter beneath the snow cover. Chipmunks were about, as were the gray squirrels, and here and there on the stems of the precious Arboretum shrubs, I could see the nipped prunings of cottontail rabbits.

A few decades after its founding, the Arnold Arboretum had thousands of species of trees and shrubs. Its researchers and plant collectors ranged the globe in search of new species for the collection, which now numbers well over 13,000—many introduced to the United States for the first time by the Arboretum. The grounds were laid out by Frederick Law Olmsted, but the real father of the Arboretum collection was Charles Sprague Sargent.

Like so many others engaged in the high moral work of Boston society, Sargent was the well-connected son of a prominent Boston banker. He was also a relative of the painter John Singer Sargent and of the radical Universalist sect member and early feminist Judith Sargent Murray. Charles, like William Brewster and other innovators around Boston, never had to work for a living and in fact was never known as a scholar at Harvard. But he did like puttering around Holm Lea, his father's Brookline estate, which had an impressive collection of laurels and rhododendrons, as well as many species of trees. Sargent took on the work of managing the grounds of the estate, became familiar with horticulture in the process, and as a result (with a little help from his friends) was appointed director of Harvard's botanical garden in Cambridge. But he had grander ambitions.

Working with Olmsted, Sargent organized a committee to create an arboretum and signed on more than a thousand supporters among the influential families around the city. It took him over twenty-five years, and he had to spend a great deal of his own money, but he managed to create the first public arboretum in the United States. He ran it for more than fifty years, and in that time assembled a collection of 6,000 species.

All these parks and seemingly sacrosanct open spaces, though apparently protected by covenants and legal restrictions, may not be as safe as we believe. Back in the 1930s, at the height of his power, the controversial Boston mayor and congressman James Michael Curley, announced that he was launching a plan to sell the city-owned Public Garden for $10 million. Fortunately, nothing ever came of that idea, and in fact part of the plan was simply bravado designed to enrage his already enraged political enemies, the Boston Brahmins, who had run the city's political system throughout its history.

Curley was the bad boy of Boston politics. Twice jailed, the so-called Rascal King altered the political system and had a major influence on the face of the city. But in spite of his self-aggrandizement and the fact that he successfully enriched himself at public expense, he did transform certain aspects of the city's environment for the better. As the self-appointed mayor of the poor, he managed to help his people by halting plans to run elevated trolley lines through poor neighborhoods. He also built schools and was able to direct federal funds to Boston for public housing. And perhaps unintentionally, he almost completed the full circle of Olmsted's Emerald Necklace.

Olmsted's planned expansion of parkland out Columbia Road to the coast never materialized, although he did build a small park at Pleasure Bay known as Marine Park. In Curley's time, the 1930s and '40s, the shoreline and mud flats between Columbia Point and South Boston were a polluted wasteland, a forgotten section of the coast often used as a dump. It was also a favorite landing area for local rum runners during Prohibition. Planners intended to give up on all the beaches in this section and create an industrial park with rail yards and warehouses. But Curley improved the parks, preserved and expanded Marine Park, and created swimming beaches all along Dorchester Bay out to Columbia Point.

When I first came to Boston to visit my brother in the 1960s, I was totally unaware of the fact that I had arrived in the middle of a major transition taking place in the city. This was a period when the old park systems and greenways of the mid-nineteenth century were under attack from all quarters. Just down the street from my brother's place, parts of the Common had been ribboned off and huge yellow dinosaurs were digging away at the sacred center of the town. This, I was told, was the work of something called the Boston Redevelopment Authority, which was in the process of creating a parking garage under the Common.

In fact, what was happening at the Common was just the latest phase in a massive remake of the city as part of what was termed the "New Boston." In the 1950s city agencies and the Boston Redevelopment Authority began the usual clearances and improvements. What this meant, generally speaking, was that the neighborhoods of the poor and disenfranchised would be cleared so that the brave new world of the automobile and the corporate high-rise could move in. It started in 1949 with the cynical obliteration of Olmsted's riverside park and the creation of Storrow Drive, and it continued with the destruction, later in the 1960s, of Olmsted's accessible and much-used oasis, Wood Island Park in East Boston, in order to expand the local airport, which had already overrun the historic Governor's Island, Bird Island, Apple Island, and all the flats in between. Highway projects slouched onward. The rough beast of the bulldozer took out row upon row of splendid old nineteenth-century buildings in the South End, thereby evicting a working community of African Americans. Then it crawled southward and drove through the city in the form of the now extinct Central Artery. This ingenious work of urban planning, a veritable Great Wall of steel girders and concrete, effectively cut the waterfront and the North End off from the city, sliced in half the tightly knit Chinese American neighborhood, destroyed more than one hundred residences, and evicted nine hundred business operations. Not only that, the highway didn't work. Layered with centipede-like on- and off-ramps that spidered down into the city from the elevated highway, it only made downtown traffic worse. And the congestion got worse decade by decade as the automobile replaced public transportation and traffic expanded to three times the highway's carrying capacity.

But that was just the beginning. In order to create the New Boston, it was also necessary to destroy an active neighborhood known as the West End, a labyrinth of narrow streets lined with butcher shops, bakeries, taverns, and crowded tenements, housing a mixed salad of Poles, Greeks, Italians, and Eastern European Jews, with a peppering of practically every other immigrant community attempting to establish itself in the city.

Under the aegis of the New Boston, developers cleared the West End, the poor were moved elsewhere, and a great Soviet-era housing block known as Charles River Park arose. (How developers have managed to associate the pleasing word "park" with high-rises and industrial buildings has always mystified me.) Ironically, given the heartless, faceless, cold, and sterile look of the "park" structures that replaced the old, historical, interesting, though squalid buildings, the new high-rises won architectural awards. Not only that, the plan—which was intended to lure the middle class back into the city—worked, and the city began to regain population.

The great Behemoth of the future rolled on, plowing under that nasty hive of depravity and perverse pleasures known as Scollay Square, which for more than a century had provided entertainment for visiting sailors and Harvard boys, and even the occasional adult Brahmin male. The beast bulldozer cleared the area, and in its place created a wind-blasted stone desert known as Government Center, which everyone, save for those forced to work there, attempted to avoid.

Then the beast lumbered onward. It constructed the 153-mile Massachusetts Turnpike, which rammed through Olmsted's Fenway at its eastern end and destroyed the old Charlesgate in the process. The great white hope of Route 128, the future "Technology Highway" of America, circled the outskirts of the city, cutting through working farms and once quiet suburbs. In 1964 Boston's first skyscraper, the fifty-two-story Prudential Tower, rose up into the New England sky, so lofty a monument to the new city that it could be seen from the heights of Mount Monadnock in New Hampshire, its scale so outrageous for the old city that one critic labeled it "urban character assassination."

All this was a tremendous amount of subsidized work. A great deal had to be torn down before the New Boston could rise up—so much that one impolitic developer, frustrated by all the wrecking that had to be carried out, announced publicly that he envied Berlin, which at least had the advantage of having been cleared by Allied bombs, making way for the bright new world. Another city councilor, a man without a strong sense of place, I daresay, suggested that it would be far better to have a shining high-rise city such as Miami or New York than the low, dark, historic buildings of Boston, even if the new buildings happened to be in a place where American history had been made.

It did seem that the architects of the New Boston were taking his advice; historic preservation, restoration of neighborhoods, and creation of new parks and green spaces were not part of the agenda. In the mad dash for the future, developers tore down, along with Olmsted-designed parks, culturally rich neighborhoods, and historic sites, such as the office of the abolitionist William Lloyd Garrison in the West End.

On my periodic visits to Boston in those years I would generally seek out what remained of the city's pleasant aspects or go over to East Boston to help my brother, although this I avoided as much as possible since it was foul work.

Over the course of the winter, under heartless conditions, in the icy winds off the harbor and the half-frozen mud of the treeless, scraped grounds of Esterhill's Yard, my brother and Eve had managed to repair the broken frames, fit on new planking, gouge out dry caulking, and then, on the few sunny days in March, scrape and sand and paint. Nearby there was a small metal-working factory, which imprisoned its workers in a dungeonlike cellar amid heavy machines that thundered and hammered daylong. Sometimes, on warmer sunny days when Eve stripped down to her minimalist short shorts and T-shirt, my brother would notice the faces of the prisoners staring up through the barred windows, longing to be free. This image of quiet desperation merely had the effect of spurring my brother to complete his houseboat project and sail away.

They labored on, redoing the exterior. On those days when icy sleet or wind or rain or snow or snow mixed with rain, or rain mixed with sleet, or a cold North Atlantic fog swept in—that is to say, on any typical early spring day in Boston—they would work inside, painting and sanding and varnishing and fitting in cabinetry.

Foul weather, new construction, and the questionable local cuisine notwithstanding, I found something comfortable about the city of Boston. There was something familiar about the place, some sense of old settled time that lingered in certain sections of the city and reminded me of Europe. Boston wasn't Florence or Rome or Paris, by any means; there were no outdoor cafés in those unfortunate decades, you could not find such a thing as an espresso, there was no wine to speak of, no yogurt, and no such thing anywhere as a croissant, as far as I could tell, and I did not have the money to dine on the American wild game and other fare served at Locke-Ober and the Ritz. But the city did remind me of Europe in some ways.

I am by no means the first one to notice this. Mary McCarthy says, in her book *The Stones of Florence*, that Boston and Florence have a lot in common: many Botticellis and Raphaels in its museums, many little shops selling post cards and tourist trinkets. Also many banks and insurance agencies. She might also have mentioned the presence of old, powerful merchant founding families and the authority of a singular religion.

Mary McCarthy's assessment may be accurate, but I would still argue for comparison with London: many narrow streets at the heart of the old city lined with residences influenced by

Robert Adam and Christopher Wren, extensive country parks, and a flat local cuisine. This comparison works for the new London as well. Both cities have been ill treated by a preponderance of high-rise construction that dwarfs and even obliterates their classic old skylines and sadly compromises their historic districts.

Boston is Boston, though. It exhibits all the elements of a city with a sense of place, a sense of itself, a deep structure that offers its residents the luxury of looking backward. The past in Boston is not really dead, it isn't even past, which is not the case in most American cities, and it is not by any means the wave of the cities of the future. In the new world that is currently abuilding, as in China and a few so-called developing countries, whole new cities are constructed in a matter of years, not a matter of centuries.

The fact is, in spite of the wreckage of the 1950s and the early 1960s, there was hope in Boston. For one thing, not all the wildlife had been evicted, as evidenced by the huge snapper I had seen in the Fenway and the swifts that would spirit past my brother's attic window on Commonwealth Avenue. And there were other signs of hope, even in the most unlikely places, such as the islands of the harbor and the neighborhoods around Esterhill's Boatyard.

The old wharf rats down at Esterhill's were a motley crew, a mix of tough old seamen and longshoremen, with a dash of college-educated boat lovers and artists, such as my brother. One of the younger denizens of this latter group was a Harvard graduate of the old Brahmin class called Muggsy, who owned a towboat named the *Priscilla*. Muggsy had somehow finagled a contract to clean sticks and driftwood from Boston Harbor, and periodically he and his friends would make periodic expeditions out to the islands to entertain themselves.

On one of these expeditions, the *Priscilla* landed on Spectacle Island, and a small group put ashore. This particular harbor island was named for two drumlins that, to colonial eyes ashore, resembled a pair of spectacles. It was used for a variety of purposes over the centuries, including an early offshore gambling joint. But in the 1920s the city located its municipal dump and a grease-rendering plant on the island. The dump had been closed for a few years when my brother was there in the early sixties, and the topography of the place had been altered dramatically; more than thirty acres of land had been added, and old dump fires were still smoldering beneath the surface like a latent volcano. The subterranean fires had the effect of keeping the grasses green through most of the winter.

My brother, his girlfriend, Eve, and an Englishwoman named Serena crossed the hills of the island and were sitting quietly on a rocky prominence when a healthy fox with long golden fur appeared suddenly. It fled when it spotted them, but they followed and saw it again in front of its den, its fur blowing in the salt wind like silk. As my brother wrote in a later reminiscence of his time at Esterhill's, it was difficult to comprehend how such a beautiful wild creature could live at peace near a city so bent on entering the steel and glass hallways of the future.

It should be said that the destruction of old Boston in the 1950s and '60s did not go unnoticed by the few insurgents left in the city. There had been an outcry from the residents of Beacon Hill when the news was announced that a highway was to be driven through the Esplanade. This had long had been a favorite walking place for local residents, and it was the site of the band shell, where the Boston Pops Orchestra performed on summer evenings. It was also the location of a playground.

A single Beacon Hill mother, pushing her baby carriage through the streets of the Hill, in the grand old revolutionary style of Hemenway and Hall, assembled other baby carriage–pushing mothers. Gossip spread, and as the highway proposal moved through various stages of permits, the women organized beneath the banner of Mothers Against Storrow Drive. Pushing their carriages ahead of them, the mothers marched into the marble halls of the State House, toddlers in tow, strewing cookie crumbs and wailing. They forced their way into the august offices of the governor himself and presented their case. But the best they were offered was a compromise. The city officials promised to expand the banks of the Charles into the river and to recreate the park and the shell and the playground rather than bury the whole embankment in asphalt. As it was, in the first round of voting, the bill to create the highway was defeated anyway. But the politically savvy highway forces endured and managed to push the bill through on a second try.

During an earlier renovation project, city planners had determined that the brick sidewalks of Beacon Hill were slippery and dangerous and must be replaced with cement. Beacon Hill residents, mostly women, got word of the "improvements" and halted the project by using one of the techniques of the unionists, a sit-down strike. They brought their garden furniture out onto the sidewalks and placed themselves in front of the oncoming workers, some of whom were actually supportive. At one point, a passing milkman joined the women and stretched himself across the sidewalk. The old bricks were saved.

A similar street action was used on Memorial Drive in Cambridge when the highway planners decided that the rows of old sycamores lining the river road were dangerous obstructions and had to be cut down. Local women chained themselves to the trees to prevent the work.

True to Boston form, by the mid-1960s other protests were taking place in the city to resist an escalating war in Southeast Asia in a heretofore largely unheard-of country called Vietnam. These demonstrations began to escalate over the next few years as wave after wave of students and fellow travelers descended on the Common, the standard meeting ground for such rallies. And during this same period, the old, latent ethics of Harriet Hemenway and Minna Hall began to reemerge, and a new age of conservation was born.

The Trustees of Reservations, the Massachusetts Audubon Society, local land trusts, and a flowering of newer environmental groups began acquiring open spaces all across the state, in some cases just before the bulldozers moved in. An obscure scholarly paper published in the 1960s had revealed that salt marshes, such as those that once surrounded the Shawmut, were the veritable nurseries of the sea and were critical to local fisheries. The paper also demonstrated that these wastelands acted as buffers during storms and floods. Staff at the Audubon Society knew of the studies and, with the state Department of Natural Resources, managed to have a law passed that protected salt marshes, the first such law in the nation. Then, applying the same logic to freshwater wetlands, the state passed a law protecting inland swamps and marshes.

Around that time there had been a series of major floods on the Charles, and the Army Corps of Engineers determined that the way to prevent further flooding was to build more dams in the upper reaches of the Charles River watershed—in spite of the fact that dams and mills and filled wetlands were among the reasons the river was flooding in the first place. Environmentalists arose in protest, citing studies indicating that preserving the wetlands of the watershed would be a more effective, and also cheaper, form of flood control, inasmuch as the swamps and marshes would absorb the excess waters and then release them slowly during dry periods. The Corps, after some hesitation, agreed, and huge tracts of land in the upper reaches of the Charles were preserved.

During the same period, the state passed a single overarching law, the Wetlands Protection Act, which served to safeguard all wetlands, salt marsh and freshwater alike, and the federal government, using the Massachusetts model, passed a similar law, thereby theoretically protecting all the wetlands of the nation.

The same change of thinking that had taken place with wetlands was occurring in the field of wildlife conservation. Massachusetts Audubon Society members, many of whom were sharp observers of local bird life, needless to say, had noticed that robins and other songbirds were dying hideous, quivering deaths on people's front lawns. Down in Washington, the writer Rachel Carson had observed similar occurrences and had acquired a mass of data indicating that the birds were dying from pesticide poisoning. She was reluctant to publish the facts, however, knowing the firestorm her findings would ignite. The

Boston publisher Houghton Mifflin, encouraged by a young editor named Paul Brooks, had offered Carson a contract for a book on the subject, but she had resisted. Then a graphic letter from a Mass Audubon bird watcher, spelling out the aftereffects of a spraying incident, was published in the *Boston Globe* and passed on to Carson. Outraged, she finally got to work and finished *Silent Spring*, which, as she expected, created a conflagration of criticism but eventually brought about changes in federal laws regarding the use of pesticides made from toxic chlorinated hydrocarbons, which were causing all the problems.

As a result of strong state and federal laws, within a decade, threatened populations of birds such as ospreys began to return. Following this, other restoration projects were started around the state. A program to restore the endangered bald eagles, one or two of whom used to appear at Boston's huge Quabbin Reservoir in winter, managed to encourage new nesting and a return of the eagle population. Then a similar program brought back the peregrine falcons, pairs of which began nesting on the high-rise buildings of the new Boston. Other raptors, such as red-tailed hawks, adapted to the city, where they fed upon squirrels in the Fenway as well as the rats and mice of the city streets. One by one, species by species, some of the former nesting birds of the Shawmut slowly returned.

But the steamroller of highway building, aided by generous federal highway subsidies, was still moving in these decades. Following a master plan devised in the late 1940s and early '50s, at the height of auto fever, city planners called for construction of a ruinous "Inner Belt" highway system that would extend Interstate 95 north from Route 128 southwest of the city and blast through the thriving little working-class neighborhoods of Hyde Park and Jamaica Plain, then wedge directly through the South End, cut through the Fenway, cross over the Charles, and ram through Cambridge to Route 93.

In the South End section, the plans called for an immense five-story interchange that would connect with a new highway to be called the Southwest Expressway. It was an ingenious design, but it was perfectly tuned to invite resistance, proposing as it did the destruction of small neighborhoods, the eviction of poor people, the ruin of a section of the Emerald Necklace, the destruction of the Charles River viewscape, the wreckage of Cambridge, and the visual pollution resulting from a massive, swirling highway clover leaf, winding down into what was once a living city of human beings, now to be sacrificed to machines. It was classic 1950s thinking. The timing was wrong, though.

The old revolutionary spirit of Boston rose up, and an alliance of blacks, Brahmins, and Irish, plus an eclectic company of community activists, joined together to fight against the tyrant.

Needless to say, this being Boston, a protest was organized, and thousands marched to the Common under the banner "People Before Highways Day."

The people included environmentalists, housing rights types, advocates for the unemployed, supporters of public transportation, and a smattering of those willing rebels within the city who will join a protest just because it's there. All this was coupled with a great deal of pressure from committees and subcommittees, appointed and encouraged by the protesters. Eventually, the newly elected governor, Francis Sargent (a relative of the Arboretum's Charles Sprague Sargent, who was a relative of John Singer Sargent et al.), responded and ultimately canceled the project, even though it meant a substantial loss of federal funds.

The other aspect of the rising tide of environmentalism that started in the late 1960s with the defeat of the highway and the wetlands preservation victories was a new attention to the city's remnant open spaces and new park possibilities. Charles Eliot's creation, the Metropolitan District Commission, which was charged with oversight of all the public recreational and open-space sites in the city, began taking a new interest in park expansion, aided, somewhat ironically, given some of their other projects, by the Boston Redevelopment Authority, as well as other local land and garden conservation groups such as the Boston Urban Gardeners and the Boston Natural Areas Network. One by one, new parks began to appear in the city, including a five-mile-long green space in the area cleared for part of the disastrous Inner Belt proposal, the largest park project in the city since the creation of Olmsted's Emerald Necklace. Also planned and approved was an extension of Olmsted and Eliot's original river park along the Charles, which, when completed, will stretch from Boston out to Watertown Square and Route 128 in Weston, nearly six miles of riverbank. Similar conservation projects were planned along the Neponset River and the Mystic, where a 180-acre former dump site was turned into a restored waterfront park.

The new consciousness also inspired an ambitious restoration of Olmsted's masterpiece, the Emerald Necklace, which in the age of the automobile had fallen into sad decline. A long-range project that started in 1985 fixed the stone bridges and reconstructed elements of the park that had been compromised, including, in a dramatic turn of the normal course of events—the removal of a parking lot. The project improved the old Victory Gardens and restored the 1930s Kelleher Rose Garden, which in the sad decade of the 1950s had become overgrown with weeds. The new garden opened in 1997 with a celebratory high tea in the English manner (of course).

One of the most expensive efforts of these various reclamations and new parks was focused on the old Shawmut Peninsula in what is now the heart of downtown Boston. Here, in the area bordered by Chinatown on the south, Beacon Hill, City Hall, the North End, and the harbor there are no less than twenty-four small, new or refashioned parks, squares, plazas, and market centers, including Post Office Square and the hugely successful restoration of the Faneuil Hall Marketplace, which brings in more than 20 million visitors a year and has served as a model for urban restoration projects around the nation.

As I settled back into Boston that March, the memory of Savannah slowly faded and the cruel northern spring rolled on. The gray pussy willows turned to light yellow tassels that swayed in the bursts of wind. Fox sparrows arrived, and all along the Muddy River, the muskrats began building fresh mounds of mud and rushes for their nests and burrowing into the riverbanks. Late in the month the phoebes returned to the neighborhoods along the Fenway. Spring azure butterflies appeared and joined the mourning cloaks, which had been flitting around the Arboretum and the Public Garden since the first week of the month. The brambles and dogwoods and other shrubs took on a rosy hue, and in every scrap of undeveloped land anywhere within the city, spring began to reveal itself.

Then it snowed.

The wet snow descended on the city and covered the crocuses and snowdrops and coated the leaves and shoots of the daffodils and tulips in the little squares and gardens across the town. The whole environment took on a dismal hue, that old gray on gray of late winter, with cold fog mixed with something between sleet, rain, and dank, blowing snow.

And then the sun came out.

On one of the apparently fortuitous sunny, albeit untrustworthy, days, I determined to explore the pocket parks and gardens of the dark interior of the old Shawmut to see what I could see.

By midday the myriad little parks and squares were crowded with workers who had descended from their perched office cubicles. Many had purchased take-out sandwiches, and they filled the benches and curbs and spread themselves on any available green space, their jackets removed, sleeves rolled, sweaters stripped off, and faces turned upward to the glorious sun.

Wherever possible, the landscape architecture firms that had been charged with park reclamations and new creations allowed the earth to return and planted, sometimes in overly regimented rows, banks of tulips and daffodils, which now, in the glory of the hour, were nodding in the gentle breeze out of the southwest. Over in Quincy Market, part of the Faneuil Hall restoration, the flower vendors, hawkers, buskers, pedestrians, and tourists were out in full force. On weekends here, this little square attracts a diverse cross-section of people. Packs of drummers collect, as well as clowns, dancers, jugglers, fire-eaters, con men, street people, Japanese tourists, English tourists, German tourists, suburban gapers, couples of various sexual persuasions, thugs and punks, political activists, drunks, and beggars, and here and there a passing banker or businessman in a suit and tie and shiny street shoes. Once, lounging here at an outdoor café, I saw a speedy, winged form sweep down from one of the high-rise buildings, bank sharply in midair, and dash down one of the modernist dark canyons in pursuit of something. It took me a while to realize I had just seen one of the resident peregrine falcons. Pigeons, one of the foods of urban peregrines, are here in full force in all seasons, as are the starlings and English sparrows. And in the evening I have also seen, along with the gulls, circling bands of swifts, and I have heard and seen the long-winged nighthawks soaring above the rooftops.

Later that March day, after the lunch hour, with the sun well over the yardarm, I walked over to Columbus Park, part of the chain of new parks and squares running from Government Center to the waterfront. I was lounging on a sea wall near the park watching the action, when a middle-aged gentleman dressed in pressed khaki trousers, a flannel shirt, and L. L. Bean hunting boots settled near me, put his nose into the *Globe*, and began reading, turning the pages impatiently.

After a few minutes, he gave up suddenly, folded the paper, and slammed it down dramatically on the sea wall.

"This town is a ruin," he said to me, shaking his head sadly.

I had been thinking the opposite. I told him I agreed, but that at least there had been a few improvements.

"And look what they have brought us," he said, jerking his

head toward a troop of teenagers who were just then passing in back of us. They were dressed in motley—sloppy, baggy pants and jackets emblazoned with company labels—and were herded together, slouching along, feeding on ice cream.

"I remember this town when it was a lot better," he said. "The bars full of happy drunks, filthy old Haymarket spilling rotten vegetables over there, the North End run by good old Mafia families, Southie run by the Irish, and Beacon Hill was still Beacon Hill."

"Have you been away?" I asked him.

This was either the right question or the wrong question, depending on the amount of time one was willing to spend with this man. Without further prompting he launched into the story of his life.

Although he didn't say as much, he was obviously out of one of the old Proper Bostonian families, the kind of outlander eccentric that this group sometimes breeds up. He had lived in India for a while and also Southeast Asia, then had settled on the West Coast, where he had spent the last ten or fifteen years. He never mentioned his parents, but carried on about a perhaps eccentric uncle who had been in the English Department at the "university," which I took to be Harvard, and had written, as he said, *the* book on English literature. My companion had come back East to visit this old uncle, who was now ensconced somewhere in a nursing home. His main complaint about Boston was that it had been turned into a haven for young urban professionals with no character, no history, no foundation whatsoever in the liberal arts, and no identity save a certain technological ability with the demonic device known as the computer.

"And that's another thing," he said (this was a favorite seguing phrase for his monologues). "Computers. What kind of world have we created? Look at these pasty-faced nerds who have no life other than sports and computer games; that, and too much money. If you're going to have money you should know how to spend it. They should offer courses in school—'What to Do with Money.'"

This led him to the tasteless disasters of modernist architecture.

"Look what they did around the Common, with all those glass walls. Look at Government Center—devoid of all human life. Look at all the lost squares of Boston. Look at Copley Square, for Christ's sake . . ."

He leaned toward me, resting on his left arm; I thought I caught the sweet scent of alcohol on his breath. "Did you know that Copley Square—until they put that, that, THING up there, was considered one of the most perfectly balanced little plazas in the *world?* H. H. Richardson—you know him, right?"

I said I did.

"Okay. H. H. Richardson. One of the greats. Never heard of a computer, did he? And look what he built. And then along comes—what's his name—that Chinese guy"—he meant the architect I. M. Pei—"and computer money, and look what they do. No sensibility in this town anymore, no education, no history, limited visual acuity, educated by modernists, the low point in human endeavor, if you ask me—"

"Are you an architect?" I asked

"No. I studied architectural history, though. Now I just collect."

"Collect what, buildings?" I asked.

"No, no, no, my good man, not at all, Mimbres pottery. You know of Mimbres pottery?"

"Yes," I said. In fact, I knew about it only because my wife, a museum person, had told me something about it. But I didn't get a chance to tell him that.

"Yes?" he asked, surprised. "But how do you know Mimbres pottery? No one knows Mimbres pottery around here. Mimbres pottery is one of the finest achievements of art and industry ever created. Believe me. Listen, I've seen all the Raphaels of Florence and Rome. I've seen the Parthenon at sunrise, seen the Taj Mahal in moonlight, I've seen the scroll paintings of Qua Lin, but I've never seen anything so fine as Mimbres pottery. You say you know the pottery? Well, then, you know exactly what I'm talking about. It's true, isn't it? How can there be any doubt?"

I was about to tell him that my family had always taught me that the most perfect marriage of art and industry was a Boston creation—Donald McKay's slim-winged clipper ship—but before I could explain, a gull skimmed past and landed on a piling on the other side of a boat slip.

"What the hell is that?" he said. "A little gull? They shouldn't be here now, should they?"

Before I could say that I was not familiar with the migratory dates for the European little gull, he went off on another tirade, this one having to do with birds.

When he was a child in Boston, he was taken out with his uncle on Sunday bird walks around Boston and Cambridge. The two of them, sometimes accompanied by other Boston bird watchers, "mostly old ladies," he said, would range through the nearby parks and outlying woods, sometimes driving up the coast to Plum Island and Cape Ann or south to the Fowl Marshes near the Neponset.

"I still like birds. All Uncle Bill's doing. That's how I got interested."

I made the mistake of telling him I was also interested in birds.

"That so?" he asked with obvious indifference. And then he was off again on his life story.

My new friend must have been living quite well on some old Boston family trust fund, since he had found the means to join a few overseas bird tours. These expeditions, which often carry birders to the uttermost ends of the earth in search of new species for their bird lists, are not cheap, and yet he had been almost everywhere on earth: Botswana, the Antarctic, the Artic, India, where he had lived for five years, apparently without working, and up into Bhutan, where he said he had "gotten" some new species.

"I know all about birds," he said. "I love birds. I've been all over the world looking for birds, but I haven't been back here in thirteen years, and I can't remember everything. Who can? You can't remember every species you've ever seen. What is that, anyway? A Bonaparte's gull maybe? Maybe it's a mew gull. I used to see them in California."

He stood shakily and squinted out over the channel.

From what I could see, the gull was smaller than the big old herring gulls that are now the resident gulls of Boston Harbor or the smaller ring-billed gulls that appear in the region in winter. This bird was too far away for me to see any details, but it looked to me like the little gulls you see flying around harbors in Europe, where they are residents. I tried to remember a few distinguishing field marks, but it didn't matter, my friend was off on the bird species of the San Francisco Bay Area, then on to western Mexico and the dearth of wild birds along the coast.

"Used to be there were hundreds of different species. Everywhere you looked, new birds. Now nothing. You know who did that?" he asked rhetorically. "I'll tell you who did that. Tourists. Same people who destroyed Boston."

This was getting tedious, and I was just beginning to plot my escape when he turned and extended his hand and said he must be going.

"So nice to meet you," he said, with old-school gentility. "We should talk more; I think we have a lot in common, with birds and Mimbres pottery and the like, but I'm off to drown my sorrows. Actually, I have to visit my uncle, which always requires fortification."

He nodded and tilted away back toward the town.

If indeed the stories of his wide-ranging life were true, his type was not an uncommon species for Boston. The old families of this town have produced a number of slightly eccentric, often talented offspring, some of whom, such as William Brewster, have made major contributions to the study of natural history. Many of the early members of Brewster's Nuttall Club were from the old Brahmin class, and their reports on extant populations of bird species, which are still on record today, are significant additions to current ornithological studies. Others, such as John Singer Sargent, strayed into the arts. In the late 1800s Ned Warren of Mount Vernon Street on Beacon Hill went off to England, where he organized a homosexual commune and sent his Greek and Roman acquisitions home to the Museum of Fine Arts. Another child of the Hill, Harry Crosby, who hated Boston (he called it the "city of the dreadful night"), fled to Paris, where he wrote French poetry and started the influential Black Sun Press in the 1920s. Another native son, Patrick Putnam, disappeared into Africa and lived among the Pygmies for the rest of his life. He was known in the Belgian Congo as the King of the World.

I was left alone on the pier wondering what species this gull actually might be. It was still on the nearby piling, preening itself, so I walked down the quay to get as close as I could. The bird was indeed much smaller than a herring gull and had the characteristics of a ring-bill, but I thought its legs looked a little gray, or even reddish. And then I couldn't remember whether the ring-billed gull had pink legs and the larger herring gull yellow legs or vice versa, and the more I pondered, the more I began to wonder whether this was something rarer, such as a California gull, which sometimes strays this way or, perhaps more likely, a Bonaparte's gull, as my friend had said, which occurs in Boston in winter. As I was considering these elemental questions, the bird flapped off, skimming over the gray waters to settle farther offshore, where I could get no field marks whatsoever. But such is the hunt for birds; something always presents itself as an impediment.

Ring-bills were one of the species collected for the millinery trade, and by the 1890s they had been almost extirpated in the Boston area. Now their populations have sprung back and they are common—this is the gull you often see hanging around parking lots. They spend their winters along the East Coast and are often seen in Boston Harbor, where they mix in with the larger herring gulls and black-backed gulls as well as smaller groups of glaucous and Iceland gulls.

The plume trade notwithstanding, gull populations have changed along the Massachusetts coast since the early 1900s. The herring gull and the black-backed gull were rare around Boston at that time, but for a variety of reasons they moved southward from Canadian waters in the early decades of the twentieth century. Herring gulls expanded their range starting in the 1920s, and twenty years later black-backed gulls began appearing in the harbor. They may have been drawn by the presence of open dumps or by the fishing industry, which took over the port after the decline of shipping and provided a rich supply of gull food in the form of rejected fish. This expansion of the gull populations drove out the huge numbers of common and roseate terns that used to nest in the general region. The two northern species also evicted the laughing gull, which, like the ring-bill, had almost been wiped out by the millinery trade but had sprung back by the 1940s.

There is still a great deal of bird activity in Boston Harbor in winter. Huge numbers of brant and eider collect in the outer harbor. Red-throated loons, horned grebes, scoters, buffleheads, goldeneyes, red-breasted mergansers, and Bonaparte's gulls can be seen from the high towers of the financial district, if anyone cares to look, which I understand some people do. In fact, the peregrines and the red-tailed hawks, which also nest on some of the city's buildings, generate a good deal of office gossip. One pair of red-tails nested within easy view of the offices and lunch room of the august Boston Athenaeum and provided midday entertainment for the diners and visiting scholars alike. One of the birds, a female the library employees called Laura, had the habit of streaking down toward the windows as if to attack.

It turned out that Laura was a known character to state fish and wildlife officials. In the act of protecting her nest in another section of the city, Laura had apparently terrified a few people, so the wildlife catchers descended, trapped her, and carried her out to the wilds of Quabbin Reservoir, some fifty miles west of the city, and released her. She was back within a day or two and later took up with her mate at the Athenaeum, a darker-feathered red-tail named Rob.

The other great irony of urban bird life is Logan Airport, which has been termed an "accidental wilderness" by some observers because it is so rich in wildlife activity. As far as the bloodworms, sandworms, shellfish, shore birds, and people of East Boston were concerned, the expansion of the airport in the 1950s and '60s was a major environmental disaster. But it seems that northern species of birds did not mind.

Logan Airport has 2,400 acres of grassland and marsh, and even though massive jets take off every few minutes, the habitat has attracted horned larks and snow buntings in winter and, in summer sparrows and shore birds, including the upland sandpiper, an increasingly rare grassland species in the Northeast. The airport's tundralike environment has also attracted a variety of rodents, including rats, mice, and muskrats, and its surrounding salt marshes shelter great blue herons, ducks, geese, and most of the usual winter and summer residents of the harbor. The airport tundra also attracts snowy owls, which migrate down from their summer grounds in the Arctic each winter.

For some twenty-five years, Norman Smith, director of the Massachusetts Audubon Society's Trailside Museum in the Blue Hills, counted the snowies that spent the winter in Boston, and it appears that the airport is a major wintering habitat for them. Ornithologists believe there may be more snowy owls at Logan Airport at any one time than at any other place in the world—mainly because in winter the birds tend to be spread thinly all across the Arctic. The snowies are what is known in the trade as an irruptive species; that is, they migrate only when necessary to find food, so there may be very many owls at the airport one winter and very few the next. Generally speaking, as their summer food supply of lemmings dwindles in the autumn, they begin to move. Most fly south, but some may head west, and they have even been recorded moving north—wherever there is food, which may be one of the reasons they like the airport, with its variety of prey species.

Most owls are nocturnal, but along with the short-eared owl, which also appears at the airport from time to time, the snowies feed in the day. They are strong flyers and, like hawks and falcons, chase down their fleeing prey; they can even catch other birds on the wing. In fact, they'll eat almost anything. Norman Smith has seen them feeding on great blue herons and Canada geese, which are decidedly larger, as well as black ducks and even other raptors.

Of the million or so passengers who fly out of Logan each winter, very few know of these aerial battles. But that is the way of life in the city. Every day all the behaviors of savage nature, all the hunting and mating and feeding and preening and burrowing that takes place out in the wildest places on earth occur as well in Boston. But the majority of the city's residents, even those interested in nature, witness most of these seemingly exotic events only on television.

Slowly, in its inexorable way, spring came on in little sallies. It would advance slightly and then be driven away by an attack from the northeast. It would fight back with a rare eighty-degree day and gain ground in the Arboretum and the Public Garden. As the season progressed, spring charged down the Fenway, urged on by the trumpets of geese and the dawn chorus of birds, and, at night, by the calls of peepers and the trilling of toads. New reinforcements arrived daily in the treetops, first the palm warblers, then the pine warblers, then myrtle warblers and solitary vireos. At the end of April winter made a countercharge in the form of a three-day-long cold rain; the winds of war veered slowly to the northwest and carried on around the compass into the southwest, and one bright morning in mid-May, over in the Arnold Arboretum, spring arrived in full regalia. Field observers with binoculars could hear, everywhere in the trees, chips and squeaks, buzzes, trills, and chatters as wave after wave of spring warblers arrived, and the budding oaks and maples, elms, willows, and hickories came alive with darting, flitting forms: worm eaters, parulas, wheel-squeak black-and-whites, flycatchers, vireos, ovenbirds, and common yellowthroats. Then, finally, as the weeks passed, the north wind surrendered, and the season settled in.

CHAPTER SIX

The Coast Watch

Saving the Harbor

ON JUNE 10 THAT YEAR I went over to East Boston to see if I could find the location of the old Esterhill's Yard, where my brother had spent the winter restoring his boat. As often happens to me, even after thirty-five years in and around the city, I was soon lost and had to feel my way along the spit of land that makes up East Boston, trying to find the site, which my brother had told me was not far from the bridge to Chelsea.

Around Boston, things have changed decidedly over the past forty years, and as far as East Boston is concerned, it seems that they have changed for the better. In my brother's little memoir of his season in hell at the boat yard, he described the neighborhood as a squalid warren of mean streets, with rough demimonde characters living in makeshift conditions all along the shoreline. One man who lived in a small trailer in the boat yard was taken away in handcuffs by a veritable squadron of police, and although he fortunately put up no resistance, it turned out that he had a huge stash of weapons in his trailer. Gossip at the yard was that the guns were intended for shipment to the Irish Republican Army back in the old country.

There had been murders and attempted murders in the area

when my brother worked there; the Esterhills had to pay off corrupt officials to stay in business, and the streets at night were said to be dangerous. The environment was degraded, with weedy lots, dead trees, rats and pigeons, and garbage, and the oily, dark waters of Chelsea Creek were awash with islands of questionable flotsam and jetsam at each tide. Not the type of place you would choose to settle and raise a nice little family.

But starting in the late 1980s and through the 1990s, as a result of efforts driven by local community groups and supported by city and state agencies, East Boston began work on what is now the largest waterfront park north of New York Harbor. Various agencies and neighborhood organizations and design firms have created a little sailing center on the eastern shore, with shaded pavilions and a six-hundred-foot promenade planted with native, salt-tolerant species. The restored waterfront offers grand vistas out to the Harbor Islands and back to the downtown Boston skyline.

In my efforts to locate the old Esterhill's site, I found myself casting about from one side of the East Boston peninsula to the other. Since the yard was located on Chelsea Creek, I finally parked the car and began to make my way on foot, asking the locals if they knew of the place. In spite of its improvements, I was aware that East Boston is not entirely free of crime, and at one point in my quest, on a street corner, I nearly crashed into a couple of prime suspects, a man in a sleeveless undershirt, who was much decorated with violent tattoos and needle tracks on his arms, and a tough-looking woman with a drug-ravaged face. Rather than retreat I dared to ask them directions.

In spite of their appearance they became interested in my quest and said, in so many words, that they were relative newcomers to the area and that I should ask at the salesroom of a used-car lot just down the block.

Said used-car lot, I realized as soon as I entered, was probably a chop shop, a place that reconditioned stolen cars. A group of men crowded behind a counter looked up suspiciously when I came in and asked in Spanish what I wanted. As it happens, I can fake—for a few minutes—the fast-clipped accent of slangy Castilian, so I asked directions in their native tongue. This served to disarm them, and they too became concerned about my search and began chattering among themselves in their machine-gun-burst dialect. I missed what they were saying—for all I knew they could have been plotting my demise—but finally in broken English they explained that there was a park just up the street, which they thought was once a boat yard. I should go over there and walk around. Maybe some old-timer could help me, they said.

It turned out to be good advice.

Following their directions, at the edge of Chelsea Creek in the apparent location of the old Esterhill's Boatyard, I came upon a grassy park with walkways along the shoreline and a pyramid-like hill at one end, with a spiral path to the top. At the base of the hill was a small sculpture park, an almost ceremonial arrangement of boulders, each with an inscription carved in stone. I had happened upon a park honoring Donald McKay's shipyard, the birthplace of so many of the legendary clipper ships that had been the subject of the dinner conversations of my youth. Here, inscribed on the granite boulders, were the names of some of the great ships, including the *Flying Cloud*. Also set down were what appeared to be quotes from local citizens: "Good bye to Wood Island Park," one read, referring to the Olmsted park that was destroyed to make way for the airport. I followed the circular path among the stones, reading the inscriptions. The last one I came to was a vast generalization on the subject of the human experiment: "Nature Is Life," it read.

I ascended the hill and took a seat on a bench at the summit to think this over. In the surrounding grasses a few weedy wildflowers were growing—Quaker ladies and some wild tansy and Queen Anne's lace. I leaned back in the sun and gazed over the massed towers of the city and the waters of Chelsea Creek, which seemed a lot cleaner now than in the descriptions from my brother's memoir.

June had managed to work its way into the city by this time. At the edges of the unmown open areas in the park, I could see dandelions, hawkweeds, black-eyed Susans, and daisies in various stages of bloom or seed production. As is common in Boston at any time of year, gulls were wheeling overhead and the usual collection of starlings and English sparrows were feeding on the other side of Condor Street among the sumac and ailanthus trees. Had I been of a mind to do a little more exploring in those weedy lots, I'm sure I could have found signs of mice and rats, voles, moles, perhaps a toad or a green frog, and, almost certainly, a brown snake, which is almost the snake de rigueur in the city.

Insects abounded even on the hilltop where I was sitting; I could see them rising and settling in the weedy edges, backlit and glistening in the sun. At one point I saw a dark flying form dart past and disappear. Then it zipped back, hovered in front of me like a hummingbird for a few seconds, and darted off again. It was a robber fly, a predatory insect that is not uncommon in gardens, roadsides, and fields outside the city. But this was the first one I had seen in Boston. And if they were here, in this relatively manicured site, they must be everywhere in the city.

My glimpse of this insect got me thinking about dates. In my garden at home, I keep track of seasonal changes such as the departures and arrivals of birds, the blossoming of flowers, first frosts, and the hatchings of insects. This was June 10, the day when robber flies appear in my garden every year, almost without fail.

These seasonal changes are not as fixed as they once seemed. I have been watching natural events around Boston for nearly thirty years, and slowly the dates have shifted. The first hard frosts now occur in November, whereas they used to strike in early October. Insects remain active much longer than they used to, and passerine birds stay around well into autumn. But spring, curiously enough, seems to arrive later than it did twenty years ago: snow and frost in April are not uncommon. In summer the cycle seems more fixed. Treehoppers and leafhoppers appear in mid-June, the fireflies begin to flash, buttercups bloom, and the little copper butterflies appear in the garden.

All across the city that month summer was coming in. The goldfinches were decked out in their bright summer plumage, the indigo buntings were beginning to nest over in the Arboretum, I had seen bats a few nights before, twisting over the Common, and the seed keys of the red maples were clustered at the ends of drooping stems. As the inscription had pronounced, nature is indeed life, especially in June.

The inscription on the stone, I think, was meant to be a comment on the importance of the natural world, but it was also an implied protest: by destroying nature, we destroy life and, by extension, we are gradually destroying ourselves. The quote was similar to Thoreau's famous dictum "In wildness is the preservation of the world."

This has been, in many ways, the crux of the natural history of Boston. Europeans arrived on these wild shores and, without regret or reflection, following the old biblical instruction to subdue and have dominion over the earth, began to take apart the natural systems of the Shawmut Peninsula, tearing down hills and cutting down trees, killing or driving off the resident wildlife, filling the marshes and fouling the waters of the harbor and the rivers, and even polluting the once fresh sea air. Then, and not incidentally in the same decades that Thoreau and Emerson were writing, the residents of the city, having realized what they had wrought, slowly began to attempt to put the natural world back together. They passed regulations to protect birds, created new parks, and endeavored to save what was left of the wildlands at the city edges.

One hundred years later, in the 1950s, in what must easily rank as the absolute worst decade in history as far as land conservation and architectural preservation are concerned, Bostonians began to take it all apart again to honor a new biblical doctrine, this one mandated not by the Book but by the demonic automobile. Then, in the late 1970s, a mere twenty years on, it appears that the citizens once again recognized their error and began a restoration process that is still going on in our time.

The evidence lay below me in the grassy hill of the park and the arrangement of memorial stones. As usual, none of this came to pass without a fight. East Boston itself is the result of a destructive process. This section of the city, which was annexed to the town of Boston in 1636, was originally a series of five small islands in the harbor, which were subsequently connected by fill. Noddle's Island, one of the largest of the five, was originally used for cattle grazing, as were some of the other harbor islands. In 1833 the island was developed for residential and commercial uses, as was the nearby Hog Island. The most recent filling of the East Boston islands was undertaken as part of the expansion of Logan Airport, starting in the 1940s. The most controversial of these changes was the undoing of Olmsted's lamented Wood Island Park, which had been a popular gathering place, attracting as many as 40 thousand people a year until it was overrun by the airport in 1966. But there were other battles as well.

During the last airport expansion, in the 1990s, immense dump trucks passed to and fro on the narrow streets of East Boston at all hours, shaking the buildings and spewing dust and gravel and even threatening—so it was believed—pedestrian traffic. As with other Boston antihighway movements, the baby-carriage brigade turned out. Mothers of East Boston rose up, walked their carriages into the streets, and effectively blockaded the trucks until other routes could be arranged. The protest didn't stop the airport, though, a noise nuisance that continues to plague East Boston and adjacent Winthrop.

As I sat there, looking out over the waters of Chelsea Creek and thinking long thoughts on the restoration of nature in these parts, I saw the glistening back of some beast break the water's surface and slip back beneath the tide. I couldn't believe what I was seeing. I thought at first it might be a seal. In winter, harbor seals occur in the outer harbor, and for many years a half-tame seal named Andre used to hang around the New England Aquarium docks. But from what I could see, this creature looked like a porpoise, an animal I had seen off the Massachusetts coast in summer, but never in Boston, never in the squalor and shipping traffic of the Chelsea Creek that I once knew.

I learned later, after a little homework, that the animal probably was a harbor porpoise. I learned further that the park I was in, now known as the Condor Street Urban Wild, was a former industrial site that had been cleaned up and restored and redeveloped through the efforts of the Boston Conservation Commission and the Boston Chelsea Creek Action Group. I also learned that the actual site of McKay's shipyard was on the other side of the peninsula, not far from another miraculous conservation effort, the Belle Isle Marsh.

This 241-acre marsh harbors a number of local mammals and reptiles and an abundance of shellfish, invertebrates, and juvenile fish, but it is also a major Boston birding site, a closely watched haven for local coastal species. Here, along with the usual crows, jays, grackles, red-wings, goldfinches, and swallows, less common species also occur, such as the willow flycatcher, the willet, glossy ibis, and sharp-tailed sparrow, as well as terns and black ducks, dowitchers, yellowlegs, ospreys, egrets, and herons.

All these restored wild areas, along with Piers Park, a three-acre wild area known as the Rockies, and a ten-acre parcel known as the Condor Street Overlook, are part of an ambitious redevelopment—or, more accurately, undevelopment—project of the Boston Parks and Recreation Department that is intended to expand the range of wild lands in the city beyond the landscaped parks and the city's dense, built environment.

Another effort in this program was taking place on the other side of the harbor, in South Boston, with the construction of a long and ambitious linear park—the Sapphire Necklace. This will eventually provide a walking path along the entire coast of Boston Harbor, beginning at the Neponset River and running nearly forty-seven miles along the shoreline, passing the beaches, wharves, docks, and piers all the way to Chelsea Creek. The project, now approaching completion, stretches from the Kennedy Library along the beaches rescued by the Rascal King himself and includes historical signs, cafés, mini-parks, walkways, and restaurants.

Summer, a season when the city's proximity to the sea and its cooling breezes becomes an advantage, was enjoying its finest hour by this time. Excursion boats leave nightly from the various piers and wharves, ferries to the harbor islands run by day, whale-watch boats with crowds of tourists aboard head offshore, the beaches are crowded on weekends, and the outdoor cafés of Quincy Market are jammed. And on July Fourth every year, down at the Hatch Shell, the Boston Pops Orchestra holds its annual Esplanade Concert, complete with fireworks.

I went over to the Cambridge shore on the Fourth with a group of friends and jostled through the gathering herds to find a good viewing site for the fireworks.

Out on the river in the late afternoon, small craft of all species began to flock, with more vessels arriving as dusk closed in. Even by midmorning people began to collect at the Oval, just in front of the Shell, and as the day wore on, the crowds gathered on both shores, many with picnics and children. Around 8:30, as twilight settled in, the band began to play.

We had brought along food and drink and a small dog; the night was warm, and we could see the dark silhouettes of the vessels on the river. The soft air and the sounds of music drifting over the still waters made for a pleasant outing, even before the fireworks. And then the Boston Pops Orchestra struck up the first strains of the opening chords of its traditional performance of Tchaikovsky's 1812 Overture, and at the finale the first shot went up, a great starburst that illuminated the whole river and the massed towers on the Boston shore. The dog, an energetic Jack Russell terrier, began to bark at the first barrage and continued off and on throughout the bombastic shelling, enraged perhaps by this unseen, unassailable enemy. We could hear the great ending cannonade of the overture and the bells of the Boston churches and crashing chords, and by God you could all but see the bombs bursting in air and hear—somewhat ironically, given that this was an American holiday—the moving strains of the Marseillaise.

Then the real fireworks began. One after another, the shells exploded, sending showers of sparking lights down upon the assembled. Impressive though it was, I was more interested in the botanical forms that the pyrotechnicians had created. Some shells burst out in the form of florid chrysanthemums, some were white flashes of pure daisy-form light, some rockets twisted into the upper air and then descended slowly, taking on the shapes of weeping willows and throwing off baby's-breath sprays of flares and spark showers upon the dark city. There were roses and dandelion heads and flat-topped Queen Anne's lace and arching goldenrods, and it was all splendor and light, music and noise, and all the while the crowds cheered and the dark silhouettes of the vessels blasted their horns.

Even though Boston is supposed to be a Puritan city, it seems to have a very large number of celebrations throughout the year, many of them recognized as either the best or (as usual) the first in the nation. The Boston Ballet's *Nutcracker* is one of these, as is the fireworks and Pops performance on the Fourth and the Christmas Revels (actually a Cambridge event) and First Night, a New Year's Eve celebration that begins with parades and ice sculpture and performances all across the city, and ends at midnight with another splendid fireworks display.

There is a big celebration at the Common in February with ice sculpture and skating on the Frog Pond and the Lagoon. March 17 is cause for two concomitant celebrations, Saint Patrick's Day and Evacuation Day, celebrating the British abandonment of the city in 1776. These festivities are followed by the Flower Show, then another double event, Patriots' Day and the Boston Marathon on April 19, and, in May, the famous Lilac Festival at the Arboretum. Events continue through the summer and fall with the Harbor Islands festival and the Head of the Charles Regatta, the Tea Party reenactment, and a little-known celebration called Dairy Day, when cows are allowed back on the Common for one day. One could hardly imagine an ambience more unlike the cultural environment of the original city—which, under the theocracy of the Puritans, forbade even the celebration of Christmas.

Boston Common is the center for many of these seasonal festivities. And in summer, even when there are no festivals occurring, the park is active. Little children go splashing through the fountains in the old Frog Pond, people from the nearby offices stretch out on the grass and sleep in the sun, and the resident homeless collect in little groups, gossiping about the night's adventures. Vendors turn out and tourists arrive, studying maps and searching the horizon to fix their location: the Common is not a perfect square and can easily confuse those unfamiliar with the place. Everyone passes through, it seems. I saw a collection of dark-suited men proceeding through the lower reaches of the Common in a veritable phalanx one day, surrounding an older man, whom I recognized as George Bush Senior. I have seen companies of Buddhist monks in their saffron robes wandering the pathways. Years ago the pope came to the Common, and periodically there appears a troop of serious-looking horsemen and footmen known as the Ancient and Honorable Artillery Company, dressed in crisp dark uniforms and polished brimmed caps, with rifles and shining swords and many badges. The company is an old Boston military organization, established in 1638 as a militia to train men for the coming conflicts. Every year on the first Monday in June, they march up from Faneuil Hall to the Granary Burying Ground near the north end of the Common to honor their ancestors, lay a wreath at the grave of their founder, and march on down Tremont Street with much pomp and circumstance. With so many events and demonstrations taking place around the Common throughout the year, no one pays much attention.

June is June everywhere in the world, especially in this cold coastal city where the winter sea maintains a chill hand over the peninsula well into spring. But finally the sun, the great rolling mother of all nature, rises earlier and earlier and higher and higher in the north until, on the twenty-first it breaks above the Atlantic horizon in full radiance at five in the morning and doesn't set over Arlington Heights and the western hills until eight-thirty in the evening.

There is no season in which more things burst forth: flowers, baby birds and mammals, tadpoles and toads and salamanders, insects, young snakes, and fresh green grasses. Everything rejoices in the long light: the marsh wrens are at work in the Fenway; the painted turtles and snapping turtles around Jamaica Pond and the Muddy River have laid their eggs in sandy banks; the elders and mapleleaf viburnums foam over with sprays of blossoms; the sumacs spear into the sky with green terminal spikes; the arrow-wood and shinleaf bloom; wild strawberries and blackberries and wild grapes and nightshades strew along overlooked walls in Franklin Park and Allandale Woods; and baby woodchucks and squirrels and raccoons and possums, skunks and cottontail rabbits abound. There are tanagers in the trees above, and orioles and buntings in the brush, and warblers and cuckoos, swallows and nighthawks and swifts in the sky, and on and on into July and well into full summer with lacewings at the porch lights of Jamaica Plain and Hyde Park, and bees on the magenta flowers of the thistles and on meadow rue and Saint Johnswort and pyrola in the woodlands. None of this would you know were you bounded by the interior canyons of the old Shawmut. But the fact is, Boston still has a remnant countryside just beyond the office windows of the high-rises.

There is a generally uncelebrated little park just southwest of the Arboretum in Jamaica Plain, known as Allandale Woods. It was acquired by the city in 1975 by the Urban Wilds project and was part of an overall plan with the pleasing sobriquet "the Charles to the Charles corridor." The idea was to create an eight-mile stretch of parkland and wetlands, including the Fenway, that would run from the Charles River, through to the Saw Mill River marshes, and back to the great curve of the Charles in West Roxbury.

Allandale Woods lies within easy striking distance of the offices of the Arboretum and as a result has been studied by botanists more carefully than some of the other open spaces in the city. It seems that the little ninety-acre urban wild is the last truly natural tract within the official confines of the city. The land here was once farmed; all the original trees were cleared, and in fact the woods are still interspersed with old stone walls, one of which was constructed as a make-work project in the New Deal era. After the farm was abandoned, the forest sprang back, and now maples, beech, red oak, and bitternut hickory, which would have been found on the Shawmut before it was cleared, are abundant. It is likely that the American chestnut grew around here as well. Botanists have surveyed the tract and have found that the alien and invasive plants that have overrun many sections of forest and open lands around Boston have not yet made it into the interior of Allandale Woods. Nonetheless, the perimeter of the tract is plagued by alien invaders such as garlic mustard, and because the woods are close to the Arboretum, some decidedly exotic trees have made their way over to the forest, including a few Asian cork trees.

Under the 4,000- or 5,000-year dominion of the Eastern Woodland people, these hilly woods, which are interspersed with puddingstone outcroppings, was probably just another hunting area, although given the presence of small streams, the Indians may have fished in the area and may have burned the forest to encourage the blueberries and the deer herds. Blueberries still grow in some sections of the woods.

The historical documentation of the tract begins early in

Boston history. John Winthrop granted a 275-acre plot of land, of which Allandale Woods is a part, to one Captain Joseph Weld in 1637. Weld's brother farmed the property, using African slaves and Indians as hands, and grew apples, tobacco, corn, rye, and hay. In the nineteenth century the land was sold to Benjamin Bussey, who owned the property that became the Arnold Arboretum. Later other parts of the tract were taken for the parkway that connects the Arboretum with Franklin Park. This was, in modern times, an urban empty lot, and by the 1920s, when the area was more or less urbanized, kids from the surrounding neighborhoods used to go into what they called "the Big Woods" for a variety of reasons, some, although unrecorded, no doubt unseemly. Children built fires and attempted to hunt squirrels; some of the locals jettisoned their trash there and probably arranged surreptitious trysts from time to time in spring when the birds were singing and the trout lilies and bloodroot and columbine were blooming on the forest floor. People still have the nasty habit of dumping trash around the gates, and even into the 1970s the local kids had any number of hideouts and secret camps and clubs. But that's life in the few sizable tracts that are left wild and unpatrolled in urban areas. These small untended open spaces, no matter how rough around the edges, have often been the inspiration for young naturalists. When you grow up on the streets, anything that is not lawn or manicured park seems a wilderness.

Plant surveys of the woods have found a variety of oaks, including the chestnut oak and white, black, and red oaks. Trees that favor light woods and open areas, such as sassafras, black cherry, aspen, and gray birch, grow in the small clearings, and lily of the valley and other common wildflowers, including Indian pipes, which appear in July, and sarsaparilla grow in the interior. Generally, the wildflowers of the woods are those associated with human disturbance, such as hawkweeds, goldenrods, yarrow, and asters and butter-and-eggs. There are a few good old native American wildflowers in the woods, though, such as bastard toadflax, false indigo, and yellow gerardia.

On one of those glorious summer days in mid-July, I decided to walk from the John F. Kennedy Library and see how far along the new Boston Harbor Walk I could get before wearing myself out. I went out to the library, parked my car, packed some water, binoculars, a towel, and my bathing suit, and set out through the little park below the library, which, I noticed, had been landscaped with *Rosa rugosa*, bayberry, and black pine—all plants Kennedy would have known from Cape Cod. Wide, curving stairs dropped down to the waterfront and a walkway that leads back toward the city, which you can see in the distance across Dorchester Bay.

It was not far from here, on Dorchester Heights, that George Washington set up a fort in a single night and mounted cannons that had been hauled all the way down to Boston from Fort Ticonderoga on Lake Champlain, a strategic move that eventually drove the British out of the city in 1776. All along the walk there are plaques detailing historical accounts of events surrounding the Revolutionary War. Interspersed with the signs are access points to the bay, where on this hot morning a few fishermen were gathered.

At one point on the inland side of the walk I saw an interesting little untamed and unmanicured open space, and I asked a small Asian man with a long fishing pole if he knew anything about it.

He shrugged apologetically. No English.

I walked on and came upon a crew cutting brush in the strip and asked them. Again no English, so I tried Spanish, which worked, save that they knew nothing at all about the place. They had been sent here to clear out the brush, they said. I noticed that they were in the process of cutting alien shrub species, leaving the larger native trees—a good sign. In fact, the whole area was interesting, half developed with new structures, apparently restored older buildings, some cleared landscaped parklands, and more work in progress. I grew more curious.

Onward then, passing runners, whom I dared not stop in their determined courses, a young man with a Mohawk, dressed all in black with a mean-looking chain at his waist, whom I dared not address for fear of my life, and then two ladies in print shirtwaist dresses and running shoes. They were not familiar with the area either, having wandered here from the Kennedy Library and Museum while their husbands were inside inspecting the Kennedy family artifacts and documents. They were from the Midwest, they said, and knew nothing about Boston. But they were mightily impressed by the bay and the vistas, the screaming gulls, and the fresh salt air coming in off the open sea beyond the harbor.

"Back in Iowa," one of them said, "we don't get views like this."

I continued on, and when I came to the first beach, I decided to go for a swim. Down on the shore, a young woman in a tiny bikini was walking slowly through the shallows, staring down into the waters. I didn't know about the swimming in this section—no one was in the water—so I wandered over and asked her about the water conditions.

"Good," she said, "but I'm wondering if those jellyfish are around here."

She looked down again. I noticed that she had a most interesting appearance: Caucasian features but silky black hair and Asian eyes that were bright blue, and she had a tattoo of bird wings rising above her bikini top and wore an inordinate number of silver earrings.

This was July, and having spent a little time on the waters of New England, I knew, or thought I knew, that jellyfish don't get up to these northern areas until August, and even then don't often make it above Cape Cod. I told her as much.

"But what about the invasion?" she asked.

The "invasion," she explained, had occurred a week or so back. Huge Portuguese man-of-war jellyfish had been washing up on the southwestern beaches of the Cape, stinging children and sending people to the hospital. She had seen a report on the news.

Perhaps distracted by her tiny bikini and interesting tattoo, I began an uncharacteristic lecture on the natural history of the jellies of Boston Harbor and Dorchester Bay, of which I actually knew very little. I told her that as far as I knew, the southern jellyfish, such as sea nettles and the Portuguese man-of-war and the like don't generally make it above Cape Cod because they hate cold water, although harmless species such as moon jellies, as well as ctenophores, the small bioluminescent species that are so beloved by the right whales of Massachusetts Bay, do appear in August. Further, there are any number of jellylike invertebrates in the harbor at all seasons, but you wouldn't necessarily notice them because they do not sting.

"What are you," she asked, squinting into the sun, "some kind of marine biologist or something?"

I realized I had probably gone on too long with my jellyfish speech.

"No, it's just that I have spent some time on various beaches over the years and have noticed jellyfish."

"Weird," she said.

"Weird?" I asked. I wondered if she meant me or the jellyfish, some species of which are indeed weird.

"That you know all that."

"I know—some of them are really bizarre. There's one, the lion's mane jellyfish—I think it comes down here sometimes—it's an Arctic species, and it's got these huge tentacles, one hundred feet long, and can deliver a terrible sting. In fact I think they can kill you . . ." I stopped myself.

"You mean that thing might be around here?" she asked, horrified.

"No, no, I didn't mean that. It's an Arctic species, loves cold water."

"Yeah, but you just said that those southern ones don't come up here because they hate cold water, so it's one or the other?"

"What I mean is the lion's mane does not normally occur in Boston Harbor, and neither do the sea nettles or the Portuguese man-of-war, but that doesn't mean they never come here, and so . . ."

I stopped again. She was lifting her lip in disgust.

"What I mean to say is that it's okay to swim, less danger here north of the Cape. No danger. In fact I think I'll go in."

"You sure?"

"It's okay," I said and went up the beach and dumped my pack. She watched with interest as I returned and waded into the water.

"You going to do it, then?"

"Yes," I called back.

"You're going to actually go out there and swim?"

"Yes, I'll be all right. It's safe."

She watched me for a while and then walked on, still searching the waters.

The water was shallow here, and I had to wade far out into the bay before I could actually swim, and, with no jellyfish in sight, once in deeper water I set out along the coast in a slow four-beat crawl. I could see the young woman back on the shore, looking out at me, shading her eyes. Seeing her, I remembered that I had left my bag on the beach, and that with no one else around, Mr. Mohawk might easily be on his way back and might help himself to the contents of my pack, including my binoculars, so I turned and swam back.

I sat on the beach for a while, drying off in the sun and meditating on the incredible resilience of the living things that inhabit salt water, including the local jellyfish.

I remembered an incident that I once experienced at Kelly's Landing in South Boston, as I was coming back on the boat from Thompson Island. On some long-forgotten night, rowdy street kids had stolen a shopping cart from one of the nearby grocery stores, rolled it down the ramp, and sent it spilling off the end of the dock, where it languished in the deep water for a year or so. Just as the boat pulled in to the landing, harbor workers were fishing out the cart after its sleep beneath the waters. They heaved it up onto the dock, where it stood, covered with marine life and glistening in the spring sun. A biology teacher and his students had been on the island that day, and now the teacher took the opportunity to deliver a lesson. The class gathered around as he sorted through the various species that had taken hold.

The shopping cart had become a veritable reef, lush with diverse species. Bit by bit the teacher described the wealth of living forms that could find a footing even here in the urban waters of the city. There were crabs and sponges, young mussels, amphipods, hydroids, barnacles, and many of the approximately six hundred species of invertebrates, mollusks, crustaceans, and seaweeds that currently live in Boston Harbor.

This event had taken place back in the late 1980s, when Boston Harbor was still suffering some of the worst years in its history. The old Boston shell game of covering things up and moving pollutants from one place to another had finally caught up with the enclosed waters of the harbor and had created a nationally recognized cesspool, so corrupted and foul that it had been used as political ammunition in the 1988 presidential campaign against the Democratic candidate, Massachusetts' Michael Dukakis.

One hundred years earlier, in the 1880s, the waters of the harbor had been improved by the construction of a sewage treatment plant of a sort on Moon Island, on the south side of the bay. A mile-and-a-half-long tunnel was bored through the ancient bedrock slates and conglomerates beneath Dorchester Bay, and sewage was pumped out to granite holding tanks. The disposal system was simple. Twice a day, massive floodgates were opened to allow the outgoing tide to carry the raw sewage out to the outer harbor—the out-of-sight out-of-mind system, basically. In the nineteenth century it worked well enough. The waters of the harbor improved, and the swimming beaches along the bay were opened. The only problem was that the Boston population was growing.

In spite of the fact that new sewage treatment plants were constructed on Nut Island and Deer Island, by the mid-twentieth century the harbor water quality was declining dramatically. By the 1970s the pipes to the old plants were leaking, groundwater was infiltrating, and nearly 2,000 pounds of toxic pollutants were pumped into the harbor every day. Beach closings due to bacterial contamination were common. About 1,800 shellfish beds around the city were closed, and another 2,000 were suspect and open only to commercial harvesters, who had to send their clams to purification plants.

But the story of the city, with its rise and fall of environmental conditions, is also the story of the harbor. In 1982 Senator William Golden of Weymouth, backed by an effective coalition of politicians, judges, and environmentalists, filed a suit against the city to clean up the harbor, and after many hearings and back-room decisions and proposals and counter-proposals, a new, state-of-the-art sewage treatment plant was constructed on Deer Island. Ironically, it was this generally positive environmental move that brought out the protests from the Muhucanuh Indian Confederation, which gathered in 1996 to remember and honor the Indians who had died on the island in 1675.

Deer Island did not have an illustrious history, save for its earliest years, when it was leased to one Thomas Temple, who among other claims to eminence, was a descendant of Lady Godiva. The island was so named because the early settlers on the Shawmut noticed that deer would swim out there to escape the wolves on the mainland. After Temple died, the island was used as the internment camp for the Christian Indians, then became a sort of Ellis Island for Irish immigrants, many of whom arrived here sick and debilitated from the famine and the sea voyage. A hospital was built to treat them, but more than eight hundred succumbed and are buried on the island in unmarked graves. For a while there was an almshouse on the island, and then, in the nineteenth century, a sewage treatment plant was built, the first of three, the last of which now ranks as the second largest such plant in the United States. Its cluster of egg-shaped sludge digesters serve as harbor landmarks, which you can see from the air as you fly in and out of Logan Airport.

Partly because of the Indian protests, there are still some sixty acres of open space on the island, with pathways and a two-mile trail that circles the shore, passing the burial grounds close by the huge shells of the digester eggs. The place has had an odd and questionable history, but at least the waters of the harbor are now swimmable.

I was packing my things to leave the beach and carry on toward the city when I noticed that my car keys were no longer in the backpack. I checked all my pockets, looked in the pack again, searched the sand, rechecked, and then sat down to think how to get myself out of this mess. I tried to remember where I had last seen the keys, rechecked, for the fifth or sixth time, the contents of my backpack, and then discovered a hole in one of the outside pockets. Somehow, somewhere, the keys must have slipped out.

I leaned back on my elbows and looked out at the peaceful

harbor, the blue waters, green islands beyond, and the white gulls sweeping here and there. What possible hope could there be of finding my keys again? But then, I reasoned, what could I lose by going back? So, like an old Massachusett Indian tracker, I slowly returned, my eyes sweeping the ground at every step.

I was able to remember the various spots where I had bent to look at a wildflower or read one of the historical plaques, and about halfway back to the Kennedy Library I came to a concrete planter where I remembered resting to take a drink of water. Sitting there in the same spot was a tall African American man who had just ended a long run. Before I could even ask if he had seen a set of keys in the area, he held them up.

"You looking for these?" he asked, laughing.

He handed them over, and we fell into conversation, first about the day and the heat and so on, then about his running habits, and finally about the changes that had taken place in these parts.

I had noticed at the beginning of the walk a generally pleasing, low-rise housing project interspersed with flowering trees and units with small front terraces facing the bay, which I assumed, given the view, must be a relatively pricy piece of real estate for Boston. This, I learned from the running man, was part of the Harbor Point Housing revitalization. Since we were nearby, I asked if he lived there.

"Not anymore," he said. "But I used to when it was Columbia Point."

For many who lived in more fortunate parts of the city, or even in the distant suburbs, the very name "Columbia Point" used to suggest danger. In the 1970s and into the '80s it was one of the highest-crime areas in the whole city. I had no idea it was so close.

"That's Columbia Point?" I asked, incredulous.

"Once was," he said, "until they blew it up."

The Columbia Point project was part of the urban renewal program that took place in the 1950s. The point of land had been a fetid dump, and development of the tract might have been a good thing had the planners done something other than put up a Soviet-block of cliff walls. Here, according to my source, lived drug lords, crooks, con men, murderers, and perverts of every variety known, plus a few old pensioners who lived in terror of the streets. Murders, drug deals, robberies, and assaults were commonplace.

"You'd hear gunfire in there at night. Common as barking dogs. There was a time," he said, "when firemen wouldn't go in there unless they had a police escort, and the police wouldn't ever go in alone; they had to come in force. You'd see them—lights blazing, guns drawn. You had to wonder who was more dangerous, the punks or the police. Guys were pushing dead cars off the banks right here. Throwing trash. Even dead bodies. Whitey Bulger [the notorious Boston archcriminal] used to dump his victims around here somewhere. Got worse and worse, and then my mother, she got us out just before it hit bottom. Then they blew it up and put up those condos."

I later learned that the original Columbia Point project had something like 1,500 apartments, but no one wanted to live there, and by the 1980s the place was so dangerous that only 350 units were occupied. The Boston Housing Authority gave up and leased the land to a new developer who, following the trends of the new urbanism, put up a villagelike complex. A phoenix rose from the ashes of the old dump and the dark towers, and now Harbor Point, which still offers a percentage of low-income units, is filled.

"There's a park in there," my friend said, "little sidewalks, trees. I know people living there who moved out of Columbia Point early on and then came back."

He looked up at a gull that swept past and followed it out to the bay with his eyes.

"Nice," he said.

"So what do you do," I asked, "come back here to run, now that it's safe?"

"You bet, brother. Body is the temple of the soul," he said.

Which is to say, I suppose, that nature is life.

Back in the 1960s, when Columbia Point was beginning its decline, and scandals were plaguing the city, and the harbor was a veritable cesspool of filth, my brother's friend Muggsy acquired the contract to clear floating detritus from the waterfront and the bridge abutments, which was about as much pollution control as the city seemed able to muster at that time. He would steam out of Chelsea Creek in his old towboat, *Priscilla,* clear logs and floating boards around the piers and bridges, then spend the rest of his time cruising around the harbor with a boatload of attractive women, sometimes accompanied by my brother and Eve.

Down in Esterhill's Boatyard, Eve and my brother were finally finishing up the painting and varnishing. The boat was caulked, the planks replaced, the frames strengthened; in effect, she was ready to sail. The only problem was that the *R. H. Dana* still lacked an engine. This was not an issue as far as my brother was concerned. His plan was to have Muggsy tow the boat to Martha's Vineyard, where he would anchor in Tashmoo Pond and spend the summer painting.

On a late spring day, the snowy, iced mud of Esterhill's Yard having dissolved into liquid mud, boats were cleared from around the *R. H. Dana,* and, without much ceremony, the yard truck, outfitted with its boat lift, maneuvered into place, hoisted the vessel, and churned through the mire to the launch site. She slipped into the greasy waters of the creek, was warped around some docked vessels, and made fast to the end of the wharf—essentially ready to sail and waiting for a tow.

Though I missed the launching, I did get up to Boston that month to spend a few days with a friend named Ann, a music student who wanted to attend a friend's recital at the Longy School of Music in Cambridge. We had no place to stay, so we slept on the hard floors at my brother's place without benefit of so much as a sheet or pillow. That night was warm, and I remember that a few mosquitoes made it in through his open windows—yet another nature surprise to me, as I never expected mosquitoes in the midst of city streets.

The next day we wandered around the city, killing time. Down on Commonwealth Avenue and out in the Fenway, the trees were in full leaf, people were lounging along the Charles embankment, sunbathing and strolling, and there was a fresh breeze from the east. We bought tuna sandwiches and spent the day on the riverbank in civilized entertainments before attending the debut concert in which Ann's friend was performing.

I saw people with books, reading by the river. I saw old

Brahmin types in bow ties and steel-rimmed glass, and nannies, also cut in the English style, dressed in black shirtwaists with white collars, pushing perambulators, and women with out-of-date 1940s hairdos in old-fashioned collared dresses, and students such as myself in a variety of disguises—suited up either in the style of future bankers or as downgraded budding leftists in secondhand army surplus. People with strange breeds of dogs passed us. People in each other's arms. People kissing under the trees, *à la Parisienne.* A woman on the T reading a Schubert score. Men in suits sleeping on their backs in the parks with newspapers folded over their eyes. A man juggling by the river. A crazy dancing man, with one arm waving free. Birds in the trees, big turtles in park rivers. Ducks on the river. Gulls in the sky. Boats out on the Charles like white butterflies tacking and jibing this way and that in the east wind. Also crew shells and sculls, and a kid with a guitar, sitting by the river singing passionately to no one but himself and the blue waters. Boston was, as far as I could judge from my superficial visits, a benign city.

I was of a mind to see if I could hitch a ride on Muggsy's towboat and take Ann out to the interesting islands I had seen out in the harbor. But with summer in the air, everyone at the yard was overly taxed, readying for the season and, save for the grand expedition to the Vineyard, which would consume a couple of days out of Muggsy's schedule, no one had time. But I remember sitting with Ann down by the harbor one afternoon, staring out at the mysterious islands. What could be out there, we wondered. Beaches? Seals? Pirates? Decaying forts with ghostly battalions of soldiers? And maybe a dungeon where some nefarious evildoer with wild eyes had been imprisoned for life in a dark tower? We were imaginative children and carried on with our fantasies: how we would steal a boat from Esterhill's and motor out there and land on an island topped by some crumbling castlelike edifice, and then get trapped in fog and have to spend the night, and ghosts would walk the ramparts, and eerie night birds would slip from the stone towers, and we would hear the ancient, timeless sea lapping the eastern shores relentlessly, and the moan of the distant foghorns, and then wake in the morning to a glorious sunrise, having lived through the dreadful night. I did not know then how close to reality some of these fantasies were.

To me the islands looked like pleasant offshore sites that would offer respite from the city if one were to seek such a thing in this generally easygoing town. I did not know that others had been thinking of the islands as well and that plans were forming to turn the whole collection of thirty-four islands into a national recreation area.

Nineteenth-century descriptions of the harbor islands of Boston offer an almost idyllic environment. According to old accounts, once you were clear of the smoky piers and docks and rail yards and elevators of East Boston, you could catch the first scent of the sea breezes that so refreshed those who took the frequent excursion steamers out to the shore hotels at Hull and Nantasket in those heady times. Looking northeast from Windmill Point in Nantasket or from the airy verandahs of the spacious hotels, you could view the outer islands of Brewster and Little Brewster, with the wide-open Atlantic beyond. A mile or so to the north you could see old Fort Warren on Georges Island, which every day at dawn and dusk would fire its cannon and sound off its signal bugle calls as it lowered its flag at dusk. Beyond the shore and interspersed among the islands, on any clear day, you could see the crowd of white sails of the little yachts that flitted this way and that as they tacked in and out of the harbor. Farther offshore, beyond Boston Light, on Little Brewster Island, you might catch sight of larger schooners and square-riggers, in from distant ports of call, either making sail or taking in sail as they ghosted up the Narrows between Georges and Gallops islands and rounded up past Nix's Mate to President Roads and the wharves. And plying the waters in between were steamships of the old Star Line, making for the coastal ports of Fall River or Portland, Providence or New York. From the passenger decks of one of these outbound steamships, close-hauled under the walls of Fort Warren, you could watch the green banks of the islands slipping by, and, looking back to the west from Broad Sound, with Winthrop Head to starboard and the Brewsters and Calf Island to port, you would see the glimmerglass green of the quiet inner harbor and then feel the first of the deep ocean swells. It was all light and air and the sapphire sea with green, grass-grown islands fronting the distant city.

Sailors coming into the harbor for the first time felt that the approach to the port of Boston offered one of the finest aspects of all the ports of the Seven Seas—"a glorious sail down Boston Harbor," as some phrased it. Even the writer Lincoln Colcord, who was born off Cape Horn on a ship outbound for China and lived by the sea all his life, did not pale when he depicted the arrival of a clipper ship in Boston Harbor. And no less a figure than Richard Henry Dana himself describes the excitement among the tired crewmen at the first sight of Massachusetts Bay and the familiar landmarks of the hills of home, after a hundred-and-thirty-five-day voyage around the Horn from San Diego.

One late September afternoon in 1997 I was coming back from one of the islands where the Indians once maintained their gardens and summer fishing camps. On the way into the harbor, just off the monument to Donald McKay, I saw two fireboats arching plumes of spray around a small, brown-hulled sailing craft. I looked through my binoculars and spotted what appeared to be a fifteenth-century caravel plugging along under full sail, with the clifflike towers of the Boston city skyline rising in the background. It turned out to be a replica of John Cabot's brave little vessel the *Matthew*. She was on her way home from a transatlantic passage undertaken to celebrate the five hundredth anniversary of Cabot's discovery of Newfoundland. Later that day I went aboard the *Matthew* and poked around beneath the decks, talking to the crew.

They had left Bristol Harbor in May and, having experienced fair winds, made the voyage in twenty-nine days, a few days shorter than the month or so it took Cabot—who also had fair winds on his crossing, save for a nasty gale just before making landfall. Ducking under the 'tween decks in the cramped, dank quarters, with the smell of tar and wood and bilge and hemp lines, you could get a sense of what an undertaking it was for those fifteenth- and sixteenth-century seafarers who set out to cross the Atlantic.

After 1492 they at least knew that there was dry land to the west and not some great void from which their vessels would never return. By the late 1500s, European ships began exploring the northern shores of America. Giovanni da Verrazano sailed up the New England coast in the spring of 1524, and before he returned he must have sailed past Cape Cod Bay, although he makes no mention of it. In 1602 Bartholomew Gosnold sailed into that bay and named the long arching peninsula to the southwest Cape Cod, because of the number of codfish he landed there. He even went ashore somewhere along the Massachusetts coast and found, as he writes, the ground to be full of "pease, strawberries, whortleberries" as well as "cypress" (probably larch trees) and birch, witch hazel, and beech. The waters in the bay, and presumably the harbor as well, were filled with an abundance of fish and shellfish, including, it was later reported, lobsters that weighed as much as twenty-five pounds and could be gathered into boats by hand from the shallow waters.

There were a few other expeditions after Gosnold, including a voyage by the Frenchman Sieur de Monts, in 1604, who was the first recorded discoverer of Boston Harbor. John Smith explored the coast in 1614. Then in 1625 the Anglican clergyman William Blackstone settled on the Shawmut, and five years later the *Arbella* landed.

Deep history notwithstanding, the story of the nature of Boston is not so much what it was (after all, every place was better in the folklore of things), as what it is now and what it is slated to become in the future. Currently some 3 million people live within a twenty-five-mile radius of the Harbor Islands, and ironically (perhaps not so ironically given the population), in the late 1960s and early '70s, what was once seen as a dumping ground, a wasteland, and a place to park the unwanted of one species or another was suddenly seen as a possibility, a wild, green, open space just offshore.

In 1996, after years of work and the usual round of tedious

organizational meetings, disagreements, agreements, and prolonged discussions, the city of Boston, the Commonwealth of Massachusetts, and the National Park Service managed to forge a document that would forever protect the thirty-four islands of Boston Harbor from further development. The federal Omnibus Parks and Public Lands Management Act established the Boston Harbor Islands National Recreation Area for public use and enjoyment. It was one of the most hopeful events in the environmental history of the city. Rather than another dump site, or an asylum, or a gambling casino, or a rendering plant, the plan would attempt to restore something of the character of the islands that first inspired John Smith when he put into the bay in 1614 and saw the verdant isles and the blue sea and the rows of Indian fields.

The islands are now managed by a partnership of the private sector; state and local government; and various cultural, recreational, and tourist organizations; and the Trustees of Reservations, which owns the coastal peninsula parkland known as World's End, which overlooks the harbor and was designed by Frederick Law Olmsted.

The main player in this whole gambit was an organization called the Friends of the Boston Harbor Islands, which for years worked to establish the islands in the hearts and minds of the people of the Commonwealth as a section of the world that was worth saving. Staffed entirely by volunteers, the organization ran boat trips, prepared exhibits, and held tours to encourage public appreciation of this unsung natural resource. They chose an image of the long disappeared island known as Nix's Mate for their logo. This once historically rich site (legend holds that a first mate falsely accused of murder was hung there and laid a curse on the island) has since disappeared beneath the sea. The group saw it a representative of a vanishing heritage.

From the earliest days, the harbor islands have had their individual advocates, some of them clearly misfits. One renegade, Amos Pendleton, took up residence on Grape Island and so believed in the sanctity of his retreat that he stalked the island with arms and would pepper invaders with birdshot "in inconvenient localities," as one nineteenth-century guide book politely phrased it. Pendleton, like many of the somewhat off-center characters who seem to favor Boston and its environs, was a great Munchhausen-style liar. Those who managed to gain interviews learned that he had been a smuggler on the Spanish Main before settling on his island. He also claimed to have been a slaver who would range from the coast of West Africa to Louisiana with his illegal cargo, often pursued by coastal revenuers, their cannons blazing. His refuge was a hilly island of grassy pasturage with grazing horses, the ancient shell middens of Indians, huge shore-side boulders, and a neat little vegetable plot maintained by the dangerous old hermit himself.

In more recent years, the most notable—and benign—of these guardians, without compare, was Edward Rowe Snow, who published four books on the islands and devoted his whole life to telling their history. He probably did more to promote the islands as a cultural resource and natural environment than anyone else in their unfortunate recent history, by which I mean the last three hundred years—the islands had better care and were far more appreciated when the Native Americans used them as fishing camps and gardening sites.

Over the course of his life, Snow assembled the history and

folklore of the harbor islands and was reportedly not averse to throwing in a few unsubstantiated tales of ghosts and supernatural happenings in the mysterious dungeons and subterranean stone corridors of the islands' various forts. Like many of the island buffs who have followed him, he was concerned, one might even say obsessed, with the human constructions—the forts and, especially, the lighthouses. Snow's books offer more detail on the physical structures of the harbor's great defense mechanisms than most readers would care to know. But they also offer the rich unofficial histories that make up the essence of these culturally rich little bits of high ground.

No doubt the most famous of the harbor island stories has to do with the Lady in Black, a legend promoted, and at the same time disclaimed, by Snow. During the Civil War, Fort Warren on Georges Island was used as a prison for Confederate soldiers. One of these prisoners was an officer captured at Roanoke Island just a few weeks after his marriage to a loyal and decidedly energetic southern belle. The young lieutenant was taken north and sent to dwell in the dim corridors of Fort Warren with other captives. But he somehow sent a message to his bride, describing in detail his whereabouts. His loyal wife made her way north and was taken in by a sympathetic southern family then living in Hull. One night, dressed in men's clothing and armed with a pistol, she rowed across Nantasket Roads, beached at Georges Island, and slipped past the sentries. She was then hoisted up the walls by prearranged signals and reunited with her husband.

No sooner were the two together than they began plotting their escape. They dug a tunnel under the walls but were detected in mid-dig and halted. Guards cornered the prisoners, there was a scuffle, and the invader drew her pistol, which misfired and killed her husband. Reluctantly, the commander of the prison ordered her hung as a spy. Her last request was that she be hung in women's clothes, so the soldiers searched the fort, and found some theatrical black robes. Thus attired, the perpetrator was hung. But she was not to be silenced.

Over subsequent years, guards walking the great sally port at the entrance to the fort would sometimes see fresh footprints of a woman's shoe in the snow. Later she was actually seen on the parapets by guards, some of whom shot at her. One man was court-martialed for deserting his post because of her, and another, who was climbing a ladder to the corridor of the dungeon, heard a woman's voice warning him away.

The Lady in Black is not the only ghost on the harbor islands—in fact, the old forts and barracks, stone dungeons, and corridors make excellent haunted grounds. There is, or was, a fine old dungeon at Fort Independence on Castle Island, where Edgar Allan Poe was stationed as a young man. Poe reportedly used the story of a duel that took place there as a model for his story "The Cask of Amontillado," in which, by way of revenge, a man is sealed in a wine cellar. The great granite boulders of the fort, the narrow passageways, the dank, ill-smelling interiors, and the cavelike rooms must have served as inspiration for the sealed room in the story. In a horrid example of art imitating life, or perhaps the reverse in this case, Snow claims to have met an old man on Castle Island who remembered meeting workmen who opened a section of a sealed casement wall in the fort in 1905 and found therein the skeleton of a soldier, still dressed in his antique military uniform.

Given their location, just off one of the most literate cities of the Western world, it is not surprising that the islands have influenced writers and poets, although some of these associations, it should be said, bear watching.

On a blustery September day on Little Brewster, I once met a woman dressed in a floppy wool hat, many scarves, and a long red cape, which she held tightly at the neck. She was searching the grassy heights just below Boston Light and, when I asked what she was looking for, explained that she was searching for the wildflower known as the scarlet pimpernel. I grew interested in this strange quest and offered to help. Eyes bent earthward, we began hunting the grassy verges along the walkways to the lighthouse. I was, to say the least, dubious, but I was waiting for a boat and had nothing else to do.

Some years before, the keepers of the light had adopted a mongrel dog who kept them company on the lonely winter days on the island. When the dog died in 1989, the grieving Coast Guardsmen buried her on the island and erected a crude stone marker in her memory, with a sad little epitaph: "Farah, 1977–1989, a mutt and keepers' companion for many years."

I was reading this inscription when my eyes strayed to a little red flower just to the left of the grave site—the infamous scarlet pimpernel.

My new acquaintance grew excited.

"I knew it was here," she said. "I just knew it was here." And she proceeded to explain that Baroness Emmuska Orczy, the author of the book *The Scarlet Pimpernel,* had visited these islands and had found this flower here and also on the islands off New Hampshire, and through some long, involved transference, which I couldn't quite follow (my source was one of those storytellers who rambles off into prolonged asides), the baroness decided to use this flower as the emblem of the family of the elusive hero of her novel.

Whether any of this is true I don't know. But such is the stuff of legends on these islands, and anyway, stories of this sort offer insights into the folkloric natural history that has characterized the islands in the historical period.

For example, on August 16, 1819, the prominent Boston resident James Prince was standing on the shore in Nahant, staring back at the harbor, when he saw "an animal of the fish kind" swim by. It held its head about three feet above the surface, and as it swam, its narrow back curled above the water in scalloplike loops. In short, a sea serpent.

Prince, who had a spyglass, got an excellent view of the creature as it cast back and forth along the shore. Other people out on the beach that day also saw the serpent. For the rest of that week there were many sightings, some of them by seasoned fishermen who had seen, presumably, all there is to see in the waters of Massachusetts Bay and beyond.

But one does not need fantasy to find the natural history of the islands enticing. One of the most heavily visited of the major islands is Georges, where Fort Warren is located and where, it is said, the Lady in Black still walks the ramparts. In keeping with the dark, forbidding nature of this site, she is accompanied in her nightly perambulations by that other traditional spirit of the night, the owl. One of the rarest of these is the ghostlike barn owl, which commonly resides in old buildings such as barns and bell towers. Up until the 1990s, Fort Warren had a healthy population of these denizens of the night.

Mark Primack, who was the harbor islands coordinator for the Metropolitan District Commission back in the 1980s, first became aware of the diverse owl populations of the islands when he was living year-round on Georges. One summer night after the crowds had returned to the mainland and the city lights across the waters were just blinking on, he was sitting at a picnic table just outside the fort walls when a white shape flitted silently a few feet over his head. Primack, who knew the story of the Lady in Black, bolted for the security of the nearby administration building. Once safely inside, the rational side of his mind took over and he realized, or hoped, at least, that the shape must have been an owl. Steeling himself, he went back the next night and waited. Just after dark he heard a frenetic, tinny squeaking all around him just as the shape of a giant, pale-colored owl swept by. The local rats, which also emerge at dusk to feed on the detritus left by picnickers, had seen the owl and were scurrying for cover, squealing in alarm.

After that, Primack was able to see the owl almost any night. Another evening, while he was walking the ramparts, he noticed, at eye level, the ghostly white face of one of the owls staring out from the boughs of one of the tall horse chestnut trees that had been planted some 150 years earlier by a Union officer. Later, in a tiny, boarded-up room in the fort, he found the nest. The owl's only access to the outside was a narrow loophole in the granite walls.

In a sort of moonlighting—literally—Primack began looking for owls on some of the other islands; he found more in abandoned forts on Peddocks, Thompson, and Lovells. He also found snowy and great horned owls, as well as other predatory birds, including kestrels, merlins, and sharp-shinned hawks. Ironically, these same species, as well as ospreys, glossy ibis, loons, herons, snow geese, brant, sea ducks such as the bufflehead, and many species of sparrows, can still be found around the place that was once Wood Island, now better known as Logan Airport.

In spite of its imposing stonework and ominous ramparts, bastions, and barrel-vaulted gun casements, Fort Warren provides a habitat for some seventy-two species of plants. Ancient horse chestnuts bloom each spring in the parade ground, and the so-called camp followers of Western civilization—dandelions, chickweed, ragweed, and Queen Anne's lace—grow all over the island. So do less common nonnative plants such as the scarlet pimpernel, Deptford pinks, and *Rosa rugosa.* But there are also a number of interesting native species, such as the ebony spleenwort, a lime-loving native fern that has taken hold in one of the few spots in the Boston area where it can survive. The fern grows in the mortar joints of the heavy granite walls that make up the demilune, the curving rampart of the fort. On the northwest walls, in the lime-based mortar of the seams, the spores of the spleenwort, blown in from who knows how far away, took hold and established a healthy colony. Woodfern, sensitive fern, and hay-scented fern have managed to gain a foothold on the island as well.

Read metaphorically, this natural countercharge might give one great hope. Given time and reasonable environmental conditions, plants will overtake and crumble the walls of war.

Land animals also occur on the islands, including the legendary golden fox that my brother spotted back in the 1960s. A coyote was seen at one point on Spectacle Island. Thompson has a healthy population of muskrats, and Grape Island, which has a popular camping area, is fast becoming notorious for its population of skunks. How some of the mammals arrived is a bit of a mystery. Less mysterious is the presence of rats and mice in the old fort foundations—Norway rats, deer mice, and meadow mice. They are no doubt leftovers from the days when the islands were home to sheep and cows and their accompanying supplies of grain, as well as the supplies and larder of the soldiery of the forts.

For coastal zones exposed to the sea winds, the islands have a diverse plant population. In part this is because human beings have been living and farming the islands for over three thousand years. As a result, the harbor islands have plant species that by rights should not be there. The most exotic are the trees and flowering shrubs, such as privet and mock orange, planted by a doctor who lived on Gallops Island when he was stationed there as part of the U.S. Maritime Radio School. In keeping with the island's exotic nature, there is also a resident population of domestic rabbits, all of whom are jet black. One cannot walk in this popular spot without flushing one or two of them.

Diverse nature notwithstanding, for the last 11,000 years perhaps the most common, as well as the most influential, animal to live on or visit the islands has been *Homo sapiens.* That is no less true today than it was when the Massachusett Indians first cleared the islands for their garden plots. In fact, in some ways the most enjoyable aspect of these unique land masses is the loose association of individuals who visit the islands so regularly and with such devotion as to form as sort of cult. Many of the devotees are loyal members of the Friends of the Boston Harbor Islands, but many belong to a maverick species of individualistic renegades who ever since the time of William Blackstone have quite independently associated themselves with the islands.

Go down to Long Wharf, where the water taxis and ferries depart for the various islands, on any warm weekend day and you can still see them—ex–Boston cops, fishermen, flatlanders from Kansas who came east in the summer of 1949, saw Boston Harbor, and have yet to go back to Kansas, retired bus drivers, energetic, starry-eyed younger folk who work around the wharf or on the ferries, an old cynic in a Greek fisherman's cap, a regular on the wharf who refuses to give his name whenever I dare to ask, and perhaps the most loyal of all, an older woman named Eileen who has made a point of going out to the islands every day of every weekend when the boats are running for the past twenty-five years or more. And these are just the regulars (actually, these are just the regulars that I knew—I'm sure there are others). The bulk of the visitors to the islands are those who go out at most one or two times a year and those flown in, as in days past, from other ports of call—Germany, France, Italy, Japan, the Azores, Brazil, Argentina, and beyond.

One day on one of the boats I met a full-blooded Australian aborigine, who spent most of the voyage leaning on the rails of the foredeck, staring intently at the rising islands ahead of him. "What did you see out there?" I asked him later. "Don't know," he said. "I see something afar."

I'm not sure what he meant.

Once I saw an old man, all by himself, dancing a jig on the foredeck for no apparent reason. And one day, years ago, I got caught in a serious squall in company with a craggy, bookish man carrying a rolled umbrella. On the way back to the harbor, just beyond the Georges Island jetties, the vessel lurched violently and then struggled landward in sheeting rain. The bookman stared intently forward into the deluge.

"Christ save us all from a death like this, on the rocks of Norman's Woe . . ." he quoted.

There has never been any accounting for the types that are attracted to islands, I suppose.

The defining characteristic of these islands is not the exotic plants and animals, or the history, or even the eccentric people. The defining characteristic is the ever-present sea. Here on the islands, just off one of the busiest cities on the East Coast, on almost any day you can experience a sensation close to that of wilderness. The islands offer an edge, a place apart.

To know this you have but to get out to one of the islands of the outer harbor—The Graves, for example, or one of the Brewsters—and then make your way eastward over the slicing rocks of the Permian and sit down with your back to the city. You have a whole continent behind you, and all of Europe ahead of you. And if you happen to fall into a reverie while you're there—which is not difficult to do in this place—who can blame you if you think you catch a hint of the scent of fresh-cut hay, and somewhere out there, in the mists of the summer sea, you think you spot a crowd of sail just off the shoals of the Roaring Bulls, and you hear the clank of buoys and the faint whisper of a sea chantey. And as you squint seaward, the tide rises and the east wind picks up, and suddenly the *Flying Cloud* sweeps in toward the Narrows, on her way back from a three-year round-the-world voyage with a cargo of sandalwood from Hawaii, wine from Madeira, grapes and oranges from Spain, silk and porcelain and strong black tea from China.

Back in the summer of 1962, Muggsy finally worked enough free time into his schedule to tow my brother's completed boat down to the Vineyard. By this time, on the surface at least, the *R. H. Dana* looked like a finely restored antique yacht, with a bright varnished cabin and a clean white hull, her gold-trimmed name proudly inscribed on her bow and stern. Still no engine, of course, but that didn't matter.

On a bright summer morning, lines were secured, and after some backing and filling, the old *Priscilla,* with Muggsy at the helm, towed the *R. H. Dana* down Chelsea Creek on her final voyage. Once clear of East Boston, the *Priscilla* laid a course through the islands. My brother, holding his vessel steady at the end of a long towline, watched the islands slip by as the two vessels headed out: first eastward through President Roads, passing the old shipyard of Donald MacKay, then southeast, leaving Deer Island to port, then easing south through the Narrows, with Gallops on the starboard side, Lovell to port, and then under the walls of Fort Warren on Georges and out into Nantasket Roads, where they laid a southeasterly course for the open sea, leaving the old Boston Light, Shag Rocks, Outer Brewster, and the Roaring Bulls to the north.

Soon they felt the deep swells of the open waters, and my brother could see the *Priscilla* dig in ahead of him and bury herself in a white wake, churning along like some primordial sea turtle. Slowly the smoky city, with all its squalor and hope and hard work, faded behind him. The air cleared, and the two vessels forged on, while astern the towers of Boston sank slowly beneath the horizon.

By dusk the little convoy reached the Vineyard and nosed into Tashmoo Pond, where my brother dropped anchor.

Later that summer, having developed a taste for New England waters, I joined him and spent the month of August on his boat. A few years later, after living briefly on the Vineyard, I moved up to Boston.

I made a couple of nostalgic trips out to the islands toward the end of the summer after my aborted walk along the shore. The waterfront by this time had changed dramatically. Some of the old types I had known ten years earlier who hung around the wharves had apparently moved on, replaced by a newer, perhaps healthier group of island aficionados. I went out to Fort Warren and then hopped the little interisland ferry, stopping here and there at various islands, poking around as usual.

This was mid-September, and I could see unidentifiable little fall warblers flitting through the high canopies of the horse chestnuts in the central parade ground of the fort. Out on the flats, the southbound shore birds were still passing through, blinking semaphore flashes of white wings as the flocks turned this way and that across the tidelands. The ring-billed gulls began to slip by, along with herring gulls and great black-backed gulls, and an old island watcher I met told me he had seen a seal a few days earlier. Back on the mainland, on the ridges of the Boston Basin, the red maples were just beginning to show the tinges of autumn fire. The pokeberries of the city's vacant lots were heavy with juicy purple berries; seeds and fruits of all the flowering plants of summer were full and ready to burst;

and flocks of starlings and blackbirds were casting about over the parks and greenswards. The early migrants were on their way out by then. A few weeks earlier, at dusk along the Charles, I had heard a telltale call above the Common and looked up as, one after another, migrating nighthawks swept over in the evening sky. They would carry on south over the American continent, south across Florida Bay and the Gulf, and still farther south, over Venezuela, Bolivia, the Amazon, and all the way to the uttermost end of the Americas, to Argentina, as far-ranging in their journeying as the Boston clippers once were.

Out here in the harbor, within sight of the city streets, the ancient rhythms of the seasons that the Indians knew so well were slowly turning.

On my last excursion to the islands later in the fall, waiting for the last boat back to the docks, I watched the evening sun sweep low across the western sky, silhouetting the walls of the city. One by one, as the natural light faded, the office lights flicked on and the squared and spired town turned dark as the pale rose and yellows of dusk spread north and south along the black ridges of the Boston Basin.

In spite of the cliff-dwelling nature of this contemporary city, in spite of the windy canyons of the streets and the noise and pollution and the getting and spending, the old legends of time and place still lingered there for a brief moment. Although it did not happen in the manner that he had originally expected, you could almost believe that the grand experiment John Winthrop envisioned when he and his parishioners first made a stand on this little peninsula, the prophecy of a city on a hill that could serve as a model for the world, had endured after all.

Acknowledgments

Over the years that I have spent talking to various people from various walks of life about the Boston environment, I have accumulated, along with facts and folklore, a large number of debts of gratitude. Much of the information was garnered before I even realized that a book was germinating, and for this reason any list of acknowledgments is necessarily filled with omissions. Nevertheless, I do remember and wish to thank the following people—listed in no particular order save that they were associated with an assortment of Boston-based institutions, including Harvard University and the august Massachusetts Audubon Society, which, having been part of the Boston natural history scene for more than one hundred years, proved to be my main source.

Thanks to Joe Choiniere, Chris Leahy, Simon Perkins, Wayne Petersen, Ann Prince, and Norman Smith of Mass. Audubon. Also Paul Hoffman, Richard Forman, and Larry Buel of Harvard. Sam Bass Warner, Father James Skehan, Teri Dunn, Chris Farrow, Jerry Howard, Lois Josimovich, Thomas Palmer, Richard Heath, Arleen O'Donnell, James A. Mitchell, Mark Primack, Kelly Slater, Donald Swann, Eric Radack, Fred

Contrada, Rita Barron, David Williams, Emily Hiestand, Katherine McGrath, Bartlett Harvey, Larry Millman, Tom Sullivan, Merloyd Lawrence, Bill Reiss, Roger Dell, Joe Mansfield, Jill Brown, and Ken Mallory, formerly of the New England Aquarium. All of these individuals helped give me perspective on the natural history of the city, even if they don't remember doing so.

I would also like to take this opportunity to acknowledge the uncountable number of people I met on the streets of Boston over the years whose surnames I never learned but who shared with me accounts of life in Boston, as well as stories and comparisons from far-flung ports. Some of the few whose first names I do remember have walk-on parts in the narrative, but most were anonymous.

Finally, I want to extend special thanks to Joanne Wyckoff, who encouraged me to do a book about the natural history of Boston in the first place.